NICOMACHEAN ETHICS – FOR EVERYONE

ARISTOTLE

Translated by
F.H. PETERS

Edited by
RICHARD ENLOW

FOR EVERYONE BOOKS

*For **Ohia**, who never read Aristotle but lived by his wisdom. She showed me that happiness comes from being present, joy from simplicity, and a good life is full of love, curiosity, and grace.*

ABOUT THE FOR EVERYONE SERIES

At *For Everyone Books*, we believe that the greatest ideas should be accessible to all. Learning shouldn't be a struggle —it should be clear, engaging, and, above all, useful.

The *For Everyone* series is designed to simplify and modernize classic works of philosophy, literature, and thought, making them approachable for today's readers. Each book in the series is:

- **Clear & structured** – No unnecessary detours, just the essentials.
- **Engaging & practical** – Complex ideas made easy to grasp and apply.
- **For all readers** – Whether you're a student, a life-long learner, or simply curious, these books are made for you.

We believe knowledge should empower, not intimidate. That's why we strip away the jargon, refine the lessons, and deliver wisdom in a way that speaks to everyone.

Welcome to *For Everyone Books*. Learning starts here.

A NOTE ON THE TEXT & THIS ADAPTATION

This book is a simplified version of Aristotle's *The Nicomachean Ethics*. The original text was written in Ancient Greek over 2,300 years ago. Many translations exist, but they can be hard to read. They often use old-fashioned or complex language.

This version keeps the heart of Aristotle's teachings but makes them easier to understand, using clear, modern language that removes unnecessary complexity. The goal is to make Aristotle's wisdom practical and accessible for everyone.

INTRODUCTION

What Is This Book About?

Imagine you want to get better at something—playing soccer, drawing, or being a good friend. How do you improve? You practice every day. The more you practice, the better you become.

Aristotle believed that life works the same way. If you want to be happy, wise, and good, you have to practice good habits every day. He wrote *The Nicomachean Ethics* to help people understand how to live a meaningful life.

What Is a "Good Life"?

Some people think happiness comes from having fun, making money, or becoming famous. Aristotle argued that real happiness is more than just feeling pleasure. It comes from living with purpose. It's about making good choices and being a good person. He taught that if you want to be happy, you should:

- Think carefully before making decisions.
- Find balance—not too much, not too little.
- Be kind, brave, and fair.
- Practice good habits every day.

Happiness, according to Aristotle, is not just a feeling. It's a way of living.

Why Did Aristotle Write This Book?

Aristotle wanted people to understand how to live well. He believed that being a good person isn't something you're born with—it's something you learn. Just like an athlete trains their body, a wise person trains their mind and actions. By making good choices every day, you become a better version of yourself.

What's Inside This Book?

This book will help you understand:

- What true happiness is and why it matters.
- How good habits shape your life.
- How to make smarter choices and avoid regret.
- Why being kind, fair, and brave leads to success.

WHAT MAKES A GOOD LIFE?

What Is the Greatest Good?

Everything people do has a purpose. Every skill, job, and choice is aimed at achieving something good. That's why people say that "the good" is what everything strives for.

Some goals focus on actions, like exercising to stay healthy. Others focus on results, like building a ship. When the goal is separate from the action, the result is usually more important than the action itself.

Different jobs and skills have different goals:

- A doctor aims to heal people.
- A shipbuilder aims to build a boat.
- A general aims to win a war.

Some smaller skills support larger ones. For example, making horse gear is part of horseback riding, and horseback riding is part of military strategy. In these cases, the bigger goal is more important because the smaller skills exist to serve it.

Since all actions aim at some goal, we must ask: which goal is the most important? The answer is politics, because it shapes laws and customs, guiding how people live and pursue the greatest good.

How Society Works

Every action has a purpose. So, there has to be one ultimate goal. It's something we want for itself, not just as a step to something else. If not, we would keep chasing goals but never find true satisfaction. Understanding this highest goal is like knowing exactly where to aim when shooting an arrow.

So, which field of study helps us understand this highest goal? It must be the most important subject, the one that organizes everything else. That subject is politics. Politics determines how society should be structured. It decides:

- What subjects people should learn.
- Which skills are valuable.
- What rules should be followed.

Politics includes key areas like military strategy,

economics, and public speaking. Because it shapes every aspect of life, its goal must be the greatest good for humanity.

Even if the greatest good is the same for an individual and for a whole society, achieving it at a national level is more important. Helping one person live a good life is valuable, but improving life for an entire society has a greater impact. That's why politics is such an essential study—it's about making life better for everyone.

But determining what is truly good is not like solving a simple equation. Ethics requires wisdom, and wisdom comes from experience. Just as we must train our bodies for strength, we must train our minds for virtue.

Learning from Experience

Not every subject provides clear-cut answers. Math gives exact answers, but ethics and politics rely on context. Questions about justice, fairness, and morality don't always have one perfect answer.

People also disagree on what is good. Some become rich but lose everything. Others act bravely but put themselves in danger. Because of this, we can't create rigid rules about goodness—we can only develop guiding principles.

A wise person knows that each field needs a different level of certainty. You wouldn't ask a math teacher to decide if something is fair, and you wouldn't expect a scientist to prove moral truths.

Additionally, experience is the best teacher. Political science isn't great for young people. It's not just about memorizing facts. Instead, it focuses on making smart decisions in real life. Those who are too driven by emotions struggle to learn from politics because they don't rely on reason to make choices.

It's not just about age—it's about maturity. Those who think carefully instead of acting on impulse will gain the most from studying ethics and politics.

The Search for Happiness

If politics seeks the highest good for society, what exactly is that highest good? Most people agree: it is happiness. Everyone, from ordinary folks to great philosophers, thinks that a good life means being happy.

But what exactly is happiness? People define it differently:

- Some say it's pleasure—feeling good and enjoying life.
- Others say it's wealth—having enough money to be secure.
- Some say it's success and honor—earning respect from others.

These views often change based on personal experiences. A sick person thinks happiness is health, while a poor person believes it is money. Some admire the idea that happiness is something deep and difficult to define. Some philosophers say there is one ultimate "Good." This "Good" makes every-thing else good.

We don't need to study every idea about happiness—just the most reasonable ones. But before going further, we should think about how we reason.

Since happiness is the goal of life, how do we determine what truly leads to it? Some claim wealth or pleasure, but reasoning must guide us to a deeper understanding. To reason well, we must first consider how we acquire knowledge.

How Do We Understand Ethics?

The philosopher Plato identified two ways to reason:

1 Starting from basic truths and building on them.
2 Starting with common beliefs and refining them into deeper truths.

To understand ethics and politics, we must begin with what people already know. That's why a good upbringing is crucial. If someone is raised with good habits, they already have a sense of right and wrong, even if they can't fully explain it. Studying ethics helps these people understand more. But if someone wasn't raised well, no amount of teaching will make them truly grasp goodness.

As the poet Hesiod wrote:

"The best person understands on their own. The second-best listens to wise advice. The worst person neither learns nor listens."

In other words:

- The wisest people understand things on their own.
- Those who are not naturally wise can still benefit by listening to good advice.
- But those who neither think nor listen waste their potential.

A person must either have wisdom or be willing to learn it. If they do neither, they will never reach the greatest good.

What Is the Best Life?

People have different ideas about what it means to live the best life. If we look at how people behave, we see three common ways they define happiness:

- **The Life of Pleasure** – Many people believe happiness is about feeling good. They focus on enjoyment, comfort, and fun. While this life may seem appealing, it is basic and instinctive, much like how animals live. Some rich and powerful people chase pleasure. This leads others to believe that pleasure is the greatest good.
- **The Life of Honor** – Some believe happiness comes from recognition and respect. They pursue a political

path. They seek leadership, influence, and admiration. However, honor depends on what others think of you, making it an unstable source of happiness. People seek honor because it reflects their virtue (good character and wisdom). If virtue is more important than honor, then maybe virtue—not honor—is the real key to happiness.

• **The Life of Wealth** – Some believe that money is the highest good, but money is just a tool. It has no value on its own; it is only useful because it helps us get other things. Since wealth is not a final goal, it cannot be the true source of happiness.

There is a fourth way of living—the life of contemplation (thinking and seeking wisdom)—but we will explore that later.

Do Philosophers Agree on What Is Good?

Some philosophers think there is one universal "Form of the Good." This perfect idea makes everything else good.

We should question this idea, even if it comes from respected thinkers like our teachers. As lovers of wisdom, we must value truth more than the opinions of even the most respected people.

One issue with this idea is that the word "good" is used in many different ways. We call intelligence, strength, beauty, and kindness "good," but they are all very different things. "Good" can refer to:

• A person or object (a wise leader or a strong tree).
• A quality (courage or honesty).
• A result (success or health).
• A relationship (something useful or beneficial).

Since "good" means many things, it's hard to think a single "Good" exists for all.

Can There Be One Science of "The Good"?

If there were one ultimate "Good" behind everything, there should also be one science that studies it. But in reality, different fields study different kinds of good:

• Medicine focuses on what is good for health.
• Military strategy focuses on what is good for victory.
• Gymnastics focuses on what is good for physical fitness.

Each subject focuses on its own type of good. Medicine looks at health. Military strategy focuses on victory. Ethics examines virtue. If 'goodness' meant the same thing in every case, then doctors and generals would study the same subject—which they don't. This is why a single 'Good' for everything doesn't make sense.

Also, just because something lasts forever doesn't mean it is better. A shirt that is white for one day is no less white than a shirt that stays white forever. Even if there were an eternal

"Form of the Good," that alone wouldn't make it more "good" than something temporary.

Some philosophers, such as the Pythagoreans, had unique ideas about goodness. But we won't explore those right now.

What Kind of Good Should We Focus On?

Some things are good in themselves, while others are good because they help us get something else. Intelligence, courage, and certain pleasures seem to be valuable on their own. Money, on the other hand, is only good because it helps us obtain other good things.

Saying that only the perfect "Form of the Good" is truly good makes it meaningless. No one can really experience or achieve it. We should focus on something practical, something that people can actually reach in their lives.

Some argue that knowing about "The Good" helps in daily life, like a blueprint helps a builder. But in reality, most people don't need this kind of abstract knowledge.

- A doctor doesn't need to understand "The Good"—
he just needs to know how to heal people.
- A general doesn't need to study "The Good"—he
just needs to know how to win battles.

We shouldn't chase an impossible idea of perfection. Instead, let's focus on the good that people can really achieve.

Yet, if there are so many ways to pursue happiness, does that mean goodness itself is different for each person? Or is there one absolute, universal 'Good' that defines all things?

Rather than searching for an abstract and distant 'Good,' we should focus on what actually leads to a good life. If we do so, we will find that one goal rises above all others: happiness.

What Is the Ultimate Goal of Life

Every action and skill has a goal:

- A doctor's goal is to make people healthy.
- A general's goal in war is to win.
- A builder's goal is to construct a house.

But is there one ultimate goal, something that is the final reason behind everything we do? If so, that must be the greatest good. If there are several, then the most important one is what we should focus on.

Some things are chosen for the sake of something else. For example, people want money—but not because they love money itself. They want it because it helps them get other things. The highest good must be something we choose only for itself, never as a means to something else.

Happiness seems to be this final goal.

- We choose to be happy for its own sake, not because it leads to something else.

- We seek honor, pleasure, and wisdom. We value them not just for themselves, but also because they help us find happiness.
- No one pursues happiness to get something else—it is the goal itself.

What Makes Happiness Complete?

The highest good must also be self-sufficient. This doesn't mean a person can be happy alone, without family or friends. Humans are social creatures, and happiness includes being part of a community. However, we must set limits—if happiness depended on the well-being of every person we know, we would never be able to define it.

Happiness isn't just one good thing among others. If it were, then adding even a small extra good would make something better than happiness. But happiness is meant to be the highest and most complete good. So, it must be something that makes life fulfilling on its own.

What Is the Unique Function of Humans?

Just saying "happiness is the best thing" isn't enough. We need a clearer explanation. One way to find it is by looking at the function of human beings.

Everything has a function—a purpose that defines what it is.

A flute player's function is to play the flute well. A good flute player is someone who plays skillfully.

If humans have a function, then being a good human must mean performing that function well.

So, what is the function of a human being?

- It can't be just staying alive, because plants and animals do that too.
- It can't be just sensing things, because animals also have sight and hearing.
- The unique quality of humans is reason—our ability to think and make choices based on understanding.

Thus, the function of a human must be living in a way that uses reason well.

Humans are unique because they can reason. A good life must be one where reason is used well. This is what I call virtue. It means living wisely and making just choices.

The Best Kind of Life

If the function of a human is to live according to reason, then the best life must be one where we use our reason in the best way possible. This means living with virtue—developing good habits and making wise choices.

If there are different types of virtue, then the best life is the one that follows the highest and most complete virtue. But happiness isn't something that happens in a single moment. Just as one sunny day doesn't make it summer, one good day doesn't make a person happy.

Happiness is about a lifetime of living well.

What Do People Believe About Happiness?

Now that we've talked about happiness, let's compare our idea to what people usually believe. A true idea should fit with common beliefs, while a false idea will contradict reality.

People have long divided "good things" into three groups:

• External goods – things like money, power, or good looks.
• Goods of the body – health, strength, and beauty.
• Goods of the soul – intelligence, wisdom, and virtue (good character).

The best and most important goods are those of the soul, because they come from within us. Since happiness is about how we live and act, it must be a good of the soul, not just an external thing like wealth or power.

Many think happiness links to virtue, wisdom, and pleasure. Some say happiness is one of these things, while others think it includes a mix of them. Since so many wise people have believed this, we should assume there is some truth to it.

Is Happiness About Having Goodness or Using It?

Some say happiness is about having virtue (good character), while others say it is about using it. This makes a big difference. A person can be good but do nothing—like someone who is asleep or unable to act. But if happiness is about activity, then it must involve living well and making good choices.

Think of the Olympic Games. The strongest or most beautiful athlete doesn't win the prize—only those who compete and perform well do. In the same way, the happiest people are those who actively live with goodness and wisdom, not just those who have the potential to do so.

Is a Happy Life Also a Pleasant One?

Yes! A truly happy life is also naturally enjoyable. People enjoy what they love. A horse lover enjoys horses. Someone who loves justice enjoys acting justly. A wise person enjoys thinking and learning.

For most people, different pleasures compete with each other. Someone might enjoy eating sweets but also want to be healthy, which can lead to conflict. But for a virtuous person, pleasure and goodness go together. They naturally enjoy doing what is right.

This means a truly happy life doesn't need extra pleasure added to it—it is already pleasant by itself. A person who doesn't enjoy being good isn't truly good. For example, someone who doesn't like acting kindly isn't really kind.

So, happiness is the best, most noble, and most pleasant

thing all at once. These qualities are not separate, like in the famous Greek saying:

"Most noble is that which is justest, and best is health;
But most pleasant it is to win what we love."

In reality, happiness brings all these things together into one way of life.

Does Happiness Depend on External Things?

Even though happiness comes from living well, external things still matter. It's hard to do good things without the right resources. For example:

- We need money, friends, and influence to do many noble actions.
- Beauty, good family, and children add to a good life, while their absence can make life harder.
- If someone has extreme hardships—like being ugly, lonely, or losing loved ones—it is difficult for them to be happy.

This is why some people think happiness is about good luck, while others think it's about virtue. The truth is that virtue matters most, but external things help.

Do We Learn Happiness, or Is It a Gift from the Gods?

Is happiness something we can learn, or is it given by fate or the gods? Some believe it comes from wisdom and effort, while others think it is simply a blessing. If the gods reward humans, wouldn't they give the greatest good—happiness?

Even if happiness is not sent by the gods, it still seems godlike—the best reward for a virtuous life. And if happiness comes from virtue, then most people can achieve it by living wisely and making good choices.

It's better to think happiness comes from effort, not luck. The best things in life should come from wisdom, reason, and nature, not just random chance.

Can Anyone Be Happy?

Happiness comes from living well. That's why we don't call animals happy—they don't have the ability to make good or bad choices. Even young children aren't truly happy yet because they haven't had the chance to live wisely. When people call children happy, they usually mean they have good potential for the future.

Also, happiness isn't just about one good moment—it's about a whole life. Even the happiest person can face great misfortunes. Take Priam, the king in Greek mythology. He lost everything in his old age. Someone who dies in misery is not truly happy.

So, a good life requires:

1 Virtue – being a good and wise person.
2 A full lifetime – not just short-term success.

3 Some good fortune – while not the most important, it does help.

Can We Call Someone Happy While They Are Alive?

The Greek thinker Solon said, 'Call no man happy until he is dead.' But does this mean happiness is only judged after death? That wouldn't make sense—happiness is about how we live and act.

Solon might have meant that life can change at any moment. So, we should wait until the end to see if someone lived happily. This brings up another question: Do events after a person's death affect their happiness? For example, if someone lived well but their children suffered after they died, does that make their life less happy?

This is complicated because different things affect us in different ways. It's odd to think a person swings between happiness and misery based solely on their descendants' actions. But at the same time, it would also be strange to say that their loved ones' fortunes don't matter at all.

If we judge happiness over a lifetime, can suffering cause a person to lose it? Can a truly happy person be affected by fortune, or do they remain happy despite difficulties?

A Happy Person Stays Happy Despite Life's Ups and Downs

The best way to answer this question is to go back to what we said earlier: Happiness is about living a life of virtue.

Life is unpredictable, and both good and bad things happen. Some events bring small changes, while others have a bigger impact. But a truly happy person is stable—they don't change like a chameleon just because something good or bad happens.

• Small misfortunes don't take away happiness.
• Bad luck can hurt happiness, but a good person faces challenges with strength and grace.
• In tough times, a good person stays noble. They find ways to make the best of their situation. It's like how a good general uses his army wisely or how a skilled shoemaker creates great shoes from what he has.

Yet, there are limits. When someone suffers greatly, like Priam, the Trojan king who lost everything in his old age, happiness might not last.

Can the Dead Still Be Affected by Life?

Another question is whether the fortunes of the living affect the dead. If someone's children or loved ones succeed or suffer after they die, does it change the happiness of the deceased?

Saying that the dead feel nothing seems cold and unfriendly. But saying the dead are deeply affected by the living seems strange too—since they are no longer aware of what happens. The best answer is that their loved ones' fortunes affect them only a little. It's not enough to steal their happiness or make them sad.

Happiness Is More Than Just Something We Praise

We usually praise people for being good at something—for being strong, wise, or kind. But happiness is different.

Praise is about how something compares to something else. For example:

- We praise a runner for being fast.
- We praise a just person for making fair decisions.
- We even praise the gods, though this seems odd—because it assumes we are judging them by human standards.

But happiness isn't like that. Instead of being praised, happiness is something we admire. We don't say happiness is good because of something else—happiness is good in itself.

Happiness Is the Ultimate Goal

A philosopher named Eudoxus had an interesting argument. He said we don't "praise" happiness like we do other virtues. So, that must mean happiness is higher than those things we praise. It is more like the standard by which we judge other things.

Virtue is praiseworthy because it leads to good actions.

But happiness is above praise because it is the final goal—it's what we all aim for in life.

This makes happiness the most valuable and complete thing in the world. It is the reason why we do everything else, and it is what makes life truly fulfilling.

Virtue Helps Us Live a Happy Life

Since happiness comes from living a good life, we need to understand virtue—the qualities that make a person good. The job of a political leader is to help people become virtuous and follow good laws. That's why great lawgivers, like those in Sparta and Crete, focused on teaching virtue.

But what kind of virtue are we talking about? Since happiness is about the soul, we need to focus on virtues of the soul, not just physical abilities or talents.

To understand this, we must first understand the soul itself.

The Two Parts of the Soul

The soul can be divided into two parts:

1 The irrational part – This part does not think or reason.
2 The rational part – This part does think and reason.

The irrational part has its own divisions:

• One part deals with basic life functions, like growing and digesting food. This is something all living things (plants, animals, and humans) have, so it isn't connected to human virtue.

• Another part deals with desires and emotions. Even though this part is not fully rational, it can still listen to reason.

For example, a person might desire to eat too much junk food, but their reason tells them to eat a healthy meal instead. When a person follows reason instead of just desires, they are acting wisely.

The Two Types of Virtue

Since the soul has two parts, virtue is also divided into two types:

1 Intellectual virtues - These involve how we think, reason, and understand.
Examples:
○ Wisdom (knowing deep truths)
○ Understanding (grasping ideas clearly)
○ Practical wisdom (making good decisions in life)

2 Moral virtues – These involve actions and habits.
Examples:
○ Generosity (giving freely and fairly)
○ Self-control (resisting bad desires)

○ Courage (facing fears wisely)

When we describe someone's character, we usually focus on moral virtues. We don't say, "He is wise in character," but we do say, "He is kind, patient, or brave."

Yet, both types of virtue matter. Intellectual virtues help us think well, and moral virtues help us act well. Together, they lead to a good and happy life.

Reflection & Application: What Makes a Good Life?

Reflection Questions

- What do you personally consider the highest good in life? Is it happiness, or something else?
- Do you think happiness is something we achieve, or something we practice daily?
- Have you ever pursued a goal only to realize it didn't bring the satisfaction you expected? What did that teach you?
- Which of the three common views of happiness (pleasure, honor, wealth) has influenced you the most? Has your perspective changed over time?
- How do you define virtue in your own life? Are there areas where you strive for balance?
- Aristotle suggests that political systems shape our

ability to live well. How do you see this playing out in modern society?

Actionable Steps

✓ Clarify your highest goal. Take a moment to reflect on what drives your choices. Are your daily actions aligned with what truly matters to you?

✓ Practice small acts of virtue. Each day, try to embody a virtue (courage, generosity, self-control). How does it affect your sense of happiness?

✓ Reframe happiness. Aim for lasting happiness instead of only seeking immediate pleasure. What habits or choices will bring deeper meaning to your life?

✓ Engage in thoughtful discussions. Talk with friends or family about what makes a good life. See how different perspectives shape your understanding.

✓ Observe how external factors influence happiness. See how money, status, and relationships affect your well-being. But also notice how virtue helps create real happiness.

2

MORAL VIRTUE

How Do We Become Virtuous?

There are two kinds of virtue:

1 Intellectual virtue – Comes from learning and experience. It takes time and teaching to develop.
2 Moral virtue – Comes from practice and habit. It is developed by doing good actions over and over again.

The word "ethics" comes from the Greek word "ethos," which means habit. This tells us that moral virtue isn't something we are born with—it's something we develop by practicing good habits.

For example, a rock naturally falls downward and can't be trained to float up, no matter how many times you throw it in the air. Similarly, humans aren't born naturally good or bad, but we have the ability to become virtuous through practice.

We Learn by Doing

Just like we learn to play an instrument by practicing, we become virtuous by doing good actions.

- People become brave by acting bravely.
- People become just by treating others fairly.
- People become self-controlled by resisting temptations.

This is why laws and education matter. Good laws help people build good habits. Societies with strong moral values create good citizens.

But just as practice makes a good musician, bad practice makes a bad musician. If someone constantly cheats, lies, or acts selfishly, they will form bad habits and become a bad person. So, what we do every day shapes who we are.

Finding the Right Balance

Virtue isn't about doing too much or too little—it's about finding the right balance. For example:

- A person who avoids all risks is a coward.

- A person who takes too many risks is reckless.
- A person who faces danger wisely is brave.

The same goes for other virtues. Someone who never enjoys life is dull, but someone who only seeks pleasure is selfish. A balanced person is temperate (self-controlled).

Virtue, then, is about finding the middle ground between two extremes.

Virtue Is Connected to Pleasure and Pain

A good sign that someone has developed a virtue is how they feel about doing good or bad actions.

- A just person enjoys being fair.
- A brave person feels good about facing challenges.
- A selfish person feels pain when they have to share.

People often do bad things because they enjoy them and avoid doing good things because they seem difficult. This is why training from a young age is important—we need to learn to enjoy good actions and avoid harmful ones.

Punishments also work this way. We correct people by making them feel pain when they do something wrong. Pain and pleasure influence our behavior.

Why Virtue Matters

People care a lot about pleasure—it is something we are drawn to from birth. This makes it hard to resist because it is so deeply ingrained in us. Learning to control pleasure and pain is what makes someone virtuous.

It is also harder to resist pleasure than to control anger, which is why it takes strength and wisdom to be virtuous. Mastering our desires is one of life's greatest achievements. Difficult things are often the most valuable.

The Key to Being Good

- Virtue is about pleasure and pain—we need to train ourselves to enjoy good actions and avoid bad ones.
- Virtue is developed by practice—what we do repeatedly determines our character.
- Virtue is about balance—too much or too little of anything can lead to bad character.

Happiness comes from living a good life. To be virtuous, you need effort, discipline, and good habits.

How Do We Become Virtuous?

Some people might ask: If we become just by doing just actions, doesn't that mean we're already just? If someone acts fairly or kindly, aren't they fair and kind? Just like a person who plays music is a musician.

Not exactly. Think about learning grammar. Someone might write a correct sentence by chance or by using someone else's guidance. But this doesn't mean they really grasp grammar. To be a real grammarian, they have to know the rules and apply them on their own.

Virtue works the same way. Just doing a kind or fair action once doesn't make you a kind or fair person. To truly have virtue, three things must happen:

1 You must understand what you are doing.
2 You must choose to do it because it is the right thing to do.
3 You must do it regularly so that it becomes part of who you are.

Simply knowing what is right isn't enough—many people think about virtue but don't actually practice it. It's like someone who listens to a doctor's advice but never follows it. Just like that person won't get healthy, you won't become a good person just by learning about virtue. You have to practice it.

What Is Moral Virtue?

Now, let's take a closer look at what virtue really is. Inside every person, there are three main parts that affect how we act:

1 Feelings (Passions) – These include emotions like

anger, fear, confidence, envy, joy, love, and pity. They are things we experience naturally, often without choosing them.

2 Abilities (Capacities) – These are our ability to feel emotions, like how we are able to get angry, feel excited, or be afraid.

3 Character (States of Character) – This is how we deal with our emotions. We can control them well, let them take over, or ignore them altogether.

Virtue is not just a feeling. People don't call someone "good" or "bad" just because they feel emotions. We aren't praised or blamed simply for feeling fear, anger, or happiness. Instead, people are judged based on how they handle their emotions.

Virtue is also not just an ability. Everyone has the ability to feel emotions, but that doesn't mean they use them well. We are born with the ability to feel anger or fear, but we aren't born good or bad—we have to learn how to handle these feelings the right way.

Virtue isn't just a feeling or an ability. It is a state of character. We develop it over time through practice.

Virtue Is Finding the Right Balance

Virtue isn't just a part of our character—it's what helps us be good and do good. Just like a strong eye sees well or a well-trained horse runs smoothly, a virtuous person makes good choices and lives wisely.

But how do we know what "good" looks like? In everything, there's a too much, a too little, and a just right. We call this the mean—the middle ground between extremes.

For example, the right amount of food depends on the person. An athlete needs more than someone who doesn't exercise. Virtue works the same way—it's not about picking an exact middle but finding the right balance based on the situation.

The same applies to emotions like anger, fear, or confidence. Some people feel too much, others too little. A virtuous person knows when to feel emotions, how much to feel, and how to act on them in the right way.

The same goes for actions:

- Generosity: Too much, and you give everything away. Too little, and you're selfish. The right balance is giving wisely.
- Courage: Too much, and you're reckless. Too little, and you're a coward. The right balance is bravery with wisdom.
- Self-control: Too much pleasure-seeking makes you indulgent. Avoiding all pleasure makes you lifeless. The right balance is enjoying life responsibly.

Some Things Are Always Wrong

But, not everything has a middle ground. Actions like stealing, lying, and cruelty are always wrong. You can't say, "I only stole a little, so it was virtuous." Some things are simply bad, just as courage and honesty are always good.

Applying Virtue to Real Life

Virtue isn't just a theory—it plays out in daily life:

- Courage balances fear and confidence. Too much fear = cowardice. Too much confidence = reck-lessness.
- Generosity balances saving and spending. Wasteful-ness is giving too much; greed is keeping too much.
- Self-control balances pleasure. Too much = indul-gence. Too little = not appreciating life.
- Anger must be used wisely. Some get mad over everything, while others never stand up for what's right. The right balance is good temper—getting angry at the right time, for the right reason.
- Honesty means telling the truth as it is. Boasting is exaggerating, while being overly modest hides one's abilities.
- Humor should be natural. A buffoon tries too hard, while someone who never jokes is too serious.

Why Extremes Oppose Each Other

In every virtue, there are two extremes—one of excess, one of deficiency. But these extremes don't just oppose virtue; they also oppose each other.

A brave person might seem reckless to a coward but overly cautious to someone who is truly reckless. A generous person might look wasteful to a miser but greedy to a spender.

Even though both extremes are bad, one is often worse. With courage, fear is usually the bigger problem because it stops people from acting. Indulgence is a bigger danger with self-control. Most people find it harder to resist pleasure than to avoid it completely.

Why It's Hard to Be Virtuous

Being virtuous isn't easy—it takes wisdom and practice.

Think of steering a ship. If waves push too hard to one side, the sailor leans the other way to stay on course. In the same way, if you tend to get angry too quickly, you should practice patience. If you struggle to speak up, practice confidence.

Pleasure is tricky—it can make something feel right even when it's actually harmful. That's why virtue requires wisdom and discipline, not just instinct.

In the end, finding balance is difficult, but it's the key to living a good and happy life.

∼

Reflection & Application: Moral Virtue

Reflection Questions

• What are some habits in your life that shape your character? Are they leading you toward virtue or vice?
• Can you recall a moment when you found the right balance? Maybe it was between being too timid and too bold, or too generous and too selfish.
• Are there areas where you struggle to enjoy doing the right thing? How might practice help change that?
• Aristotle says that pleasure can mislead us into thinking something is good when it isn't. Have you ever made a choice that felt good in the moment but was harmful in the long run?
• What are some things in your life that require more discipline or self-control? How could practicing virtue help?

Actionable Steps

✓ Identify one habit to improve. Pick a small goal, such as being more patient, generous, or disciplined. Focus on practicing it daily.
✓ Practice balance. If you tend to one extreme (e.g., being too reserved or too outspoken), try adjusting toward the middle.
✓ Reframe pleasure and pain. Face challenges head-on. Effort is key to lasting happiness. Find joy in doing what's right.
✓ Reflect on past choices. Think about situations

where you acted with virtue—or where you struggled. What can you learn from them?

✓ Surround yourself with good influences. Aristotle
thought that good habits arise from good surround-
ings. Seek people and situations that encourage
virtue.

3

MORAL VIRTUE (CONTINUED)

Voluntary and Involuntary Actions: Choice and Responsibility

Virtue means making good choices. But before we decide if an action is good or bad, we should ask: Did the person choose to act on their own, or were they forced?

We praise or blame people for actions they choose but forgive or pity them for actions they had no control over. This is key for grasping virtue and determining legal responsibility.

What Makes an Action Involuntary?

An action is involuntary if it happens due to force or ignorance:

• Forced actions happen when an outside force pushes someone to act, offering no personal benefit. Example: A strong wind pushes someone somewhere they didn't intend to go.
• Ignorant actions are involuntary only if the person later regrets them. If they don't feel remorse, the action wasn't truly involuntary.

Some actions fall in between—partly forced but still involve choice. Example: A sailor throws cargo overboard in a storm to save the ship. He doesn't want to do it, but he chooses to because the alternative is worse. These actions are more voluntary than involuntary. The person actively chooses to do them.

People respect those who face tough times for good reasons. But they blame those who give up too quickly, especially if they could have fought back. Some actions, like murder, are never excusable, no matter the pressure.

Can We Blame Outside Forces for Our Choices?

Some argue that people are "forced" by pleasure or desire, but this doesn't make sense. If this were true, all actions would be forced, and no one would be responsible for bad choices— only good ones. The key difference is this: Forced actions lead to regret, but actions taken for pleasure are chosen willingly.

We shouldn't blame temptations—we should recognize when we allow them to control us.

Ignorance and Responsibility

Not all ignorance excuses an action. The key is regret:

- If a person regrets their mistake, their action is involuntary.
- If they don't care, their action is still voluntary, and they bear responsibility.

Types of ignorance:

1 **Ignorance of details** – Truly involuntary if the person regrets it. Example:

- Someone unknowingly reveals a secret.
- A warrior mistakes a friend for an enemy.
- A doctor gives harmful medicine, thinking it would help.

2 **Ignorance from recklessness** – Not excusable. Example:

- A drunk person makes bad choices.
- An angry person acts impulsively.
- A cruel or greedy person claims, "I didn't know any better."

Only ignorance of the facts makes an action involuntary. Bad character or lack of self-control does not.

Are Actions Done in Anger or Desire Involuntary?

Some argue that actions driven by anger or desire should be considered involuntary, but that would mean:

- Animals and children wouldn't be responsible for anything.
- People could take credit for good actions but avoid blame for bad ones.
- Healthy actions, like eating well or learning, seem involuntary. We simply have a natural desire for them.

Anger and desire influence choices, but they don't remove responsibility. A person who lets their emotions control them is still making a choice. That's why we blame people for losing their temper or being greedy—they could have acted differently.

The Difference Between Voluntary and Involuntary Actions

- Voluntary actions come from within. The person knows what they are doing and is responsible.
- Involuntary actions happen due to force or ignorance and only if the person later regrets them.

Knowing this difference helps us decide when to praise, blame, or forgive someone.

What Is Choice?

Now that we know about voluntary and involuntary actions, let's look at choice. It is closely linked to virtue. A person's choices reveal more about their character than their actions alone.

Choice is voluntary, but not all voluntary actions are choices. Animals and young children act voluntarily, but they don't truly make choices. Some voluntary actions happen fast and require little thought. These aren't real choices either.

People sometimes confuse choice with desire, anger, wish, or opinion, but they're different:

- Choice is not desire—a person may desire unhealthy food but choose not to eat it.
- Choice is not anger—acting out of anger isn't thoughtful decision-making.
- Choice is not wishing—people wish for impossible things, like immortality, but they can't choose to be immortal.
- Choice is not opinion—opinions can be about things outside our control, but choices are about things we can act on.

Since choice isn't any of these, what is it? Choice is a careful decision. It comes after considering different options.

What Do We Deliberate About?

We don't deliberate about everything, only about things we can control and change.

- We don't deliberate about unchanging facts (e.g., the movement of stars).
- We don't deliberate about random events (e.g., finding treasure).
- We don't deliberate about other people's responsibilities (e.g., a Spartan wouldn't decide how the Scythians should govern).

We carefully consider uncertain issues, such as medicine or business. These areas have many possible solutions. The more unpredictable something is, the more we think about it. For example, sailing depends on the weather. So, people spend more time deciding about sailing than about exercising, which has clearer rules.

Choice Is About Means, Not Ends

We don't deliberate about what we want, but about how to get it.

- A doctor doesn't deliberate about whether to heal— he deliberates about which treatment to use.
- A politician doesn't deliberate about whether to

create good laws—he deliberates about how to do it best.

Deliberation is like solving a puzzle—people think step by step, working backward from their goal. If they realize the goal is impossible, they stop deliberating.

Once deliberation is complete, the person makes a choice based on their decision. That's why choice is often called "deliberate desire." It involves wanting something and thinking carefully about how to get it.

What Do We Wish For?

Wishes focus on end goals, but people don't always wish for what is truly good. Some believe people only wish for what seems good to them, while others say people always wish for what is actually good.

The truth is, the truly good is what people should wish for. But people only see what seems good to them, based on their character.

A good person sees what is truly good, while a bad person mistakes harmful things for good ones. Example: Just as some foods are truly healthy, a sick person might reject them, while a healthy person benefits from them. Similarly, a good person can recognize true goodness, while a bad person is misled.

People often make mistakes because they seek pleasure. They choose what feels good instead of what is truly good.

Virtue and Vice Are in Our Power

Since people choose their actions, virtue and vice (good and bad character) are also choices. This means we are responsible for our own moral character.

Some argue, "No one is bad on purpose." But while no one becomes happy by accident, people do become bad through their choices. If humans weren't responsible for their actions, it would mean they aren't in control of their behavior, which is clearly false.

Proof of responsibility:

• Laws punish bad actions—unless a person was truly forced or ignorant.
• Laws reward good actions—to encourage virtue.
• We don't punish people for things outside their control (e.g., feeling hungry).
• We punish carelessness. If someone breaks the law or drinks too much and commits a crime, they must take responsibility for their choices.

But what about those who claim they simply 'didn't know' something was wrong? Does ignorance excuse bad actions?

Responsibility for Ignorance

Ignorance doesn't always excuse actions:

- If someone regrets their mistake, their action was involuntary.
- If they don't care, their action was still voluntary, and they are responsible.
- Ignorance from recklessness (e.g., getting drunk and making bad decisions) is not an excuse—they chose to be careless.

People Are Responsible for Their Own Choices

Some people might say, "What if someone is just naturally careless?" Even if that's true, they are still responsible for becoming that way.

- A person who lies and cheats over and over becomes dishonest.
- A person who always looks for fun and has no self-control can be irresponsible.

Our habits shape who we are. Just like an athlete gets stronger by training, a person who keeps making bad choices becomes a bad person. If they refuse to admit this, they're just making excuses.

Can People Change Once They Have Bad Habits?

A person who keeps choosing to lie or be selfish can't say they don't want to be that way—they're making that choice every day.

But once a bad habit is formed, it's much harder to change—just like ignoring a doctor's advice can lead to an illness that's difficult to cure.

Think of it like dropping a rock. Before you drop it, you have the power to hold on. But once you let go, you can't stop it from falling.

In the same way, we can choose our actions in the beginning, but if we keep making bad choices, it gets harder to turn back.

This means being a good or bad person is up to us—our choices shape who we become.

Who Deserves Blame?

We don't blame people for things they can't control, like being born blind. But if someone ruins their health through laziness, we hold them responsible.

The same rule applies to character. If someone is born into a bad situation, they aren't to blame. But if they keep making bad choices and refuse to change, they are responsible for who they become.

Some might say, "People don't choose what looks good to them." But a person who always does the wrong thing has trained themselves to want the wrong things. A good person learns to see what is truly good.

Since we can choose to be good, we can also choose to be bad. Both are in our power.

What Is Courage?

Courage means finding the right balance between fear and confidence. It's normal to feel afraid of bad things like getting sick, being poor, or dying. But a brave person knows when fear is reasonable and when to stand strong.

For example: Fear of disgrace (shame) is a good thing—it means you care about doing what's right. Someone who doesn't care about disgrace isn't brave—they're shameless.

Fear of sickness or money problems isn't about courage—those things aren't caused by a person's character.

The greatest fear is death, because it is the end of life. But courage isn't just about facing any death—it's about facing danger for a noble reason.

The most respected form of courage is shown in battle, where people fight to protect others. That's why brave soldiers earn honor.

A truly brave person doesn't run from danger when standing firm is the right thing to do. But not every dangerous situation is the same. A sailor who stays calm in a storm isn't necessarily brave—he just trusts his skills. A brave person may not expect to survive, but they face danger with honor.

Courage vs. Fear and Foolishness

A brave person finds the right balance between fear and confidence. But some people go to extremes:

• The Reckless Person – Fears nothing, even real dangers. This isn't courage—it's foolishness.
• The Rash Person – Acts tough but backs down when real danger comes.
• The Coward – Fears too much and loses confidence. They run away instead of standing strong.

A coward is hopeless because they fear everything. A brave person has hope because they face challenges with determination.

Many rash people act fearless when there's no real danger but panic when things get serious. A truly brave person stays calm before danger but is ready to act when the time comes.

True Courage vs. False Courage

Courage is about facing fear and danger for the right reasons. A person who risks their life for a noble cause is truly brave. But some people take risks for the wrong reasons.

For example, someone who chooses to die just to escape sadness or hardship is not brave. Instead, they are running away from their problems. True courage means facing struggles, not avoiding them.

Five Kinds of "Courage" That Aren't True Courage

People often use the word "courage" for things that aren't really courage. Here are five examples of bravery that seem like courage but aren't the real thing.

1. The Courage of Soldiers in Battle

The bravery of ordinary soldiers is the closest to true courage. Many fight because they fear punishment or want honor.

In some societies, cowards are shamed, and heroes are rewarded. This pushes soldiers to be brave, even if their courage is based on fear of disgrace rather than pure virtue.

However, some soldiers fight only because they are forced to. Leaders may use threats to make them fight. True courage comes from choice, not fear.

2. The Courage of Experience

Some people seem brave because they know more than others.

• Professional soldiers stay calm in battle. They know the dangers involved.

• Their training lets them react better than regular people. It's similar to how a trained athlete outperforms a beginner.

But experience alone isn't courage. In hopeless situations, many trained soldiers flee. However, some ordinary soldiers choose to stay and fight for honor. True courage isn't just about skill—it's about standing strong even when things look bad.

3. The Courage of Anger and Emotion

Some people fight back fiercely when they are hurt or insulted. They act like wild animals—attacking out of rage, not because they've made a noble choice. Mythical heroes are often said to fight with boiling blood and fierce strength. While anger can help a brave person, it isn't the reason for true courage. Even animals fight when they are hurt or scared, but that doesn't make them brave. True courage is about thinking wisely and acting for a good cause, not just reacting with emotion.

4. The Courage of Confidence

Some people only act brave when they think they will win.

• Drunk people often seem fearless—not because they are brave, but because they don't understand the danger.

• Overconfident soldiers may fight carelessly. They think they will always win.

But when things go wrong, these people are the first to run away. True courage means facing danger even when the odds are against you, not just when you expect to win.

5. The Courage of Ignorance

Some people don't feel fear because they don't realize they're in danger. They may seem brave, but they are actually just unaware.

A group of warriors once charged into battle, believing their enemy was weak. They soon realized too late that they were badly outmatched. Once they understood the danger, they panicked and ran.

True courage is knowing the danger but facing it anyway.

Courage and the Experience of Pain

Courage is more about facing fear than feeling confident. We call people brave not because they feel strong, but because they don't give up when things are hard.

That's why courage is difficult and often painful. A boxer trains hard, takes punches, and struggles through pain just for a small reward. A brave person faces suffering and danger, not because they enjoy it, but because it's the right thing to do.

A truly good and happy person actually values life more than others, so losing it is even more painful for them. But they still choose to fight for what is right, even if it costs them everything.

Interestingly, the best soldiers aren't always the bravest. Some people risk their lives because they have nothing to lose. A truly brave person understands the value of life but still chooses to act with honor.

What Is Temperance?

With courage, we learn to manage fear. But what about pleasure? That's where temperance comes in. These two virtues help us control our impulses. One fights fear, while the other resists indulgence.

- Courage helps us face fear in the right way.
- Temperance helps us control pleasure in the right way.

The opposite of temperance is self-indulgence, which means giving in too much to pleasure.

What Kind of Pleasures Does Temperance Deal With?

Not all pleasures are the same:

- Some pleasures are of the mind, like learning new things or earning respect. These aren't physical, so people don't call them temperate or self-indulgent.
- Some pleasures are physical, like enjoying music, stories, or money. But people who love music aren't considered self-indulgent—just music lovers.

So temperance is about controlling bodily pleasures, but not all of them.

- Enjoying beautiful sights (like paintings or colors)
isn't seen as self-indulgent.
- Enjoying pleasant scents, such as flowers or incense,
isn't the same. It only counts if it's linked to cravings.
For example, you might love the smell of food
because it makes you hungry.

Even animals don't enjoy smells and sounds for their own sake. A dog loves the smell of a rabbit because it means food. A lion loves the sound of an ox because it means hunting time.

This means temperance and self-indulgence focus mostly on food, drink, and touch. These are the pleasures we also share with animals.

- A wine expert who studies flavors isn't self-indulgent, but someone who only eats for pleasure is.
- A food lover once wished for a longer throat to savor his meals. This shows that self-indulgence comes from a desire for physical pleasure.

That's why self-indulgence is seen as animal-like—it focuses on basic urges instead of what makes us human.

Self-Indulgence vs. Temperance

People have two types of desires:

1 Natural desires, like hunger and thirst—everyone has these.

2 Personal cravings, which are different for each person.

Natural desires aren't bad, but too much of anything is harmful. Some people overeat or drink too much, caring more about their stomach than anything else.

But personal cravings can be even worse. Some people crave things they shouldn't. Some crave too much of what they should have in moderation.

A self-indulgent person:

- Wants too much pleasure.
- Craves things they shouldn't.
- Feels pain when they don't get what they want.

Yes—pleasure can cause pain! A self-indulgent person suffers when they don't get their cravings.

A temperate person:

- Avoids bad pleasures.
- Enjoys good pleasures in the right amount.
- Doesn't feel pain when they don't get unnecessary pleasures.

A temperate person enjoys only what is healthy and right, without going too far.

Is Self-Indulgence Worse Than Cowardice?

Both self-indulgence and cowardice are bad, but in some ways, self-indulgence is worse.

- Self-indulgence is about pleasure.
- Cowardice is about fear.

People naturally want pleasure and avoid pain. This means controlling fear is harder than controlling desire.

Self-indulgence is worse because:

- It can lead to addiction. People find it hard to break bad habits linked to pleasure.
- Fear can make people panic and act without thinking, but self-indulgence is always a choice.

A coward may drop their weapon in battle by accident. In contrast, a self-indulgent person actively seeks pleasure, even when they know it's wrong.

Self-Indulgence and Childhood

The word "self-indulgence" is often linked to childish behavior—and for good reason! Children naturally follow their desires because they don't know better. If they aren't taught discipline, they grow into adults who only care about pleasure.

In the same way, our desires (like hunger and cravings) must be trained—just like a child needs good guidance.

A temperate person is like a well-raised child:

- They listen to reason instead of chasing every pleasure.
- They crave only what they should, when they should, and in the right amount.

This is how self-control leads to a balanced and happy life.

Next, we will explore other virtues that help us live wisely!

Reflection & Application: Choice, Responsibility, and Virtue

Reflection Questions

- Can you think of a time when you blamed circumstances for a choice you made? Looking back, how much control did you actually have?
- Have you ever done something wrong and justified it by saying, "I didn't know"? Would you still feel responsible for it?
- Aristotle says habits define our character. What

habits—good or bad—are shaping who you are right now?

• What are some pleasures you tend to overindulge in? How might practicing temperance improve your life?

• True courage means standing firm for the right reasons. Can you recall a time when you had to show courage? What motivated you to act?

• Do you think people today struggle more with fear or pleasure-seeking? Why?

Actionable Steps

✓ Take ownership of your choices. When faced with a decision, pause and ask: *Am I acting out of reason or impulse?* Recognizing control is the first step to being responsible.

✓ Reflect on a past mistake. Instead of making excuses, consider whether it was due to force, ignorance, or a personal choice. What can you learn from it?

✓ Practice small acts of courage. Speak up when you see something wrong, try something new despite fear, or stand firm in your values.

✓ Limit overindulgence. Identify one pleasure (food, entertainment, social media, etc.) where you tend to go overboard. Try cutting back and notice how it affects you.

✓ Choose a virtue to develop. Whether it's patience, courage, or self-control, find small ways to practice it daily. Habits shape character over time.

4

MORAL VIRTUE (CONTINUED)

What is Generosity

Now, let's talk about generosity, which is also known as liberality. This virtue governs how we give and receive wealth. While both matter, generosity is most admired for how one gives, rather than how one takes.

When we say "wealth," we mean anything that can be measured by money. There are two extreme ways people handle money:

- Greedy people care too much about keeping money.
- Wasteful people spend too much and don't take care of what they have.

Money is useful, so it can be used well or badly. A person with good character will use it wisely, and the best way to use money is to spend it well. A generous person does this by giving wisely instead of hoarding or wasting.

How a Generous Person Gives

A truly generous person:

• Gives to the right people, in the right amount, at the right time.
• Gives happily, not with regret.
• Doesn't just give everything away carelessly.
• Doesn't take money from bad sources.

A generous person handles their money well. This way, they can keep helping others. They do not hoard wealth out of fear, nor do they recklessly give everything away. Instead, they earn fairly so they always have the means to give.

Generosity isn't about giving huge amounts—it's about giving based on what you have. Someone with little money who still gives is more generous than a rich person who gives a lot but barely notices the loss.

Because generous people prefer giving over saving, they often don't become very rich. Some people think it's unfair that those who deserve wealth the most often get the least. This happens because they don't focus on keeping money.

Still, generosity requires balance. Giving too much or to

the wrong people is wasteful. A generous person spends wisely so they can help those who truly need it.

Wastefulness vs. Greed

Generosity is the middle ground between wastefulness and greed:

- Wasteful people give too much and take too little.
- Greedy people take too much and give too little.

A wasteful person gives away money without saving. This often leads to their downfall. Wastefulness is more common in individuals than in rulers or the wealthy. This is because rulers and the rich usually have steady income sources.

However, wastefulness is easier to fix than greed. Wasteful people can learn from poverty or age. They already like giving, so they just need to learn to do it wisely.

That's why wasteful people are considered better than greedy people—even though they do it wrong, at least they help others.

But some wasteful people also take from bad sources, just like greedy people. They can't keep up with their spending. So, they begin to borrow, gamble, or rely on flatterers. If they aren't careful, they can become selfish and careless.

Why Greed is Worse

Greed is far harder to correct than wastefulness. Unlike wastefulness, which often fades with age or hardship, greed tends to grow stronger over time. As people age, they often cling to their wealth. This makes it harder for them to be generous. Furthermore, greed is far more common than wastefulness, making it a more widespread vice.

There are two types of greedy people:

1 Stingy hoarders – They don't try to take from others but refuse to share what they have. They fear losing money, so they hoard it.
2 Money-grabbers – They take whatever they can, even from bad sources. This includes gamblers, con artists, and those who inflate prices. They care more about money than their reputation.

Not all greedy people are criminals, but some take extreme actions to get money. Thieves and con artists are the worst examples of greed because they trick and steal to get rich. People who steal from temples or cities are called wicked, not just greedy.

Because greed is both more harmful and more common, it is considered worse than wastefulness. Wasteful people may be reckless, but greedy people hurt others to get more for themselves.

What Is Magnificence?

Magnificence is a virtue of grand and meaningful spending. Generosity is for everyday gifts. Magnificence is all about investing in important things in a big way. This includes public works and grand celebrations.

A magnificent person spends money in a way that is grand and fitting for the occasion. What counts as "grand" depends on the situation:

Paying for a warship is much more expensive than organizing a festival, but both can be magnificent if done properly. What matters is not just how much is spent, but how wisely and beautifully it is spent.

Someone who spends wisely on small things isn't called magnificent—that word is for people who spend well on big things.

The Difference Between Magnificence, Generosity, and Wastefulness

A magnificent person is always generous, but not all generous people are magnificent. Generosity means giving with care. Magnificence, on the other hand, is about spending in a grand way that inspires awe.

A generous person might give money to a local school. This helps buy supplies so students have what they need. This is admirable, but it is not magnificent.

A magnificent person, however, might fund a new school building. It would have an inspiring design and a lasting impact. Their spending is not just helpful—it is extraordinary and fitting for their means.

A stingy person, on the other hand, refuses to spend even when they should. A wasteful person spends a lot of money without thinking. They often buy things just to show off to others.

A magnificent person spends like an artist. They use their wealth to create something truly meaningful and lasting. A magnificent person spends wisely. They make sure their money goes toward a noble goal. The result should be impressive, matching or exceeding the amount spent. Their goal isn't to save money or be the cheapest—it's to create something truly amazing.

What Does a Magnificent Person Spend Money On?

Magnificence means spending on things that inspire awe. It is most often seen in:

- Religious buildings and festivals
- Public projects that benefit the community (like funding a play or paying for a warship)
- Special occasions can be weddings, hosting important guests, or giving big gifts.

A great person doesn't just spend for themselves. They spend to help others and create something good. Even giving gifts can be an act of magnificence, like donating a beautiful statue to a temple.

They want their home to show their wealth and status. So, they spend money on things that last. Durability makes everything more beautiful.

Who Can Be Magnificent?

A person must have enough resources to be truly magnificent. A poor person cannot afford large projects, and if they try, they may look foolish for spending beyond their means. True magnificence comes from wealth, status, or a strong reputation. These people can spend in ways that match their position.

But, even smaller things can be magnificent if they fit the moment. A beautifully crafted toy could be a magnificent gift for a child, even if it isn't expensive. What matters isn't just the cost, but whether the result is impressive and appropriate.

What Magnificence Is Not

Wasteful people spend too much in the wrong way. They might throw an ordinary dinner party but make it as expensive as a wedding, just to show off. They waste money on things that aren't really important, yet they may still be stingy when real generosity is needed.

Stingy people are the opposite—they are too focused on saving money, even when they should be spending. They might put money into something important but ruin it by cutting corners on the final details. They think twice about every cost. They often choose the cheapest option, even when paying more is better.

The Importance of Magnificence

Neither wastefulness nor stinginess is as harmful as some vices because they don't directly hurt others. But, a truly magnificent person knows how to:

- Spend wisely
- Create beauty
- Be generous in a way that inspires admiration

In the end, magnificence is about spending money in a way that leaves a lasting, positive impact.

What Is Pride?

Pride is the virtue of recognizing one's true worth and claiming what is rightfully deserved—neither more nor less. A truly proud person believes they deserve great things, and they actually do. A vain person asks for more than they deserve. A humble person, on the other hand, deserves greatness but won't acknowledge it.

The proud person stands between these two extremes. They aim high but stay balanced, accepting only the honor that matches their true worth.

Pride and Honor

Pride is most closely tied to honor, the highest reward people give for noble actions. A truly proud person seeks honor, but only when it aligns with their true merit—they do not chase empty recognition.

- A vain person expects more honor than they have earned.
- An overly humble person expects less than they deserve.
- A truly proud person knows their worth and seeks honor only when it matches their achievements.

Since only the best people deserve the highest honors, a truly proud person must also be good. In fact, pride is often seen as the "crown" of all virtues—it enhances them and makes them shine. But true pride is rare because it requires both great character and nobility.

How a Proud Person Acts

A truly proud person does not let success make them arrogant or failure make them despair. They do not chase wealth or power just to impress others, nor do they overvalue honor itself. Since they expect to be honored for their achievements, they are not overly impressed by praise.

Some people act proud simply because they are rich or

powerful, but true pride comes from virtue, not status. Those who only imitate pride often:

- Look down on others unfairly.
- Demand respect without earning it.
- Act superior while lacking real achievements.

A truly proud person, however:

- Treats important people with dignity but does not put down those of lower status.
- Faces great risks when necessary but does not seek out danger for no reason.
- Is generous, preferring to give rather than receive.
- Repays kindness with even greater generosity.
- Does not ask for favors, beg for sympathy, or dwell on small problems.

They are also open about their feelings, expressing love and hatred honestly. Hiding emotions just to please others is beneath them, and they do not flatter or seek approval. They do not hold grudges because they do not take insults seriously, nor do they gossip or boast. Since they see very few things as truly great, they are not easily impressed by others.

Pride vs. Vanity vs. Humility

Pride is about claiming honor in a way that fits one's true worth.

- A vain person seeks excessive honor. They think too highly of their skills and focus too much on looks.
- An overly humble person denies their own worth, avoids challenges, and misses out on greatness.

Both are mistakes, but excessive humility is worse. It keeps people from reaching their full potential.

A truly proud person, on the other hand, knows their worth and lives in a way that reflects it. But what happens when people actively seek honor? This brings us to ambition —the drive to attain recognition and success.

The Virtue Between Ambition and Lack of Ambition

There's a balance between being too generous and too stingy with money. The same goes for seeking honor. Some people are too ambitious—they chase honor too eagerly, even from unworthy places. Some people are not ambitious enough— they refuse honor, even when they deserve it.

People admire ambitious people for their boldness and drive for greatness. They also value unambitious people for their humility. Because of this, ambition can seem good or bad, depending on the situation.

The problem is that the virtue between ambition and lack of ambition doesn't have a clear name. That's why people sometimes argue whether ambition is good or bad. But like all virtues, there must be a middle ground—a balanced way to pursue honor.

A person with the right amount of ambition doesn't crave

honor too much but also doesn't ignore it when they deserve it. This balance may seem slightly ambitious or slightly unambitious at times, but it is the right way to live.

Good Temper

Good temper means having the right balance when it comes to anger. Some people get angry too easily, while others never get angry at all, even when they should.

A good-tempered person:

- Gets angry at the right time, for the right reasons, and at the right people.
- Controls their anger rather than letting it take over.
- Is not vengeful and usually forgives others.

People who never get angry, even when something is clearly wrong, may seem weak or afraid. If someone never stands up for themselves or their friends, others might not respect them.

On the other hand, some people hold onto anger for too long or express it poorly:

- Quick-tempered people get mad fast but also calm down quickly.
- Sulky people keep their anger bottled up and stay mad for a long time. They only feel better if they get revenge.

- Bad-tempered people hold grudges and refuse to forgive.

We believe it's better to be calm than angry. However, the best way is to find balance. Get angry when needed, but don't let anger take over. Since it's hard to measure exactly how much anger is "just right," people must use good judgment in each situation.

Friendliness

In social situations, people act in different ways. Some people try very hard to please others. They agree even when they shouldn't. They put getting approval before being honest. These people are known as flatterers. Some people are too rude—they argue constantly and don't care if they hurt others.

The best way to act is somewhere in the middle. A truly friendly person:

- Knows when to agree and when to stand up for what is right.
- Is kind and fair but doesn't go along with something that is dishonest or harmful.
- Treats everyone with respect, even strangers.

Friendliness is not the same as friendship. It doesn't stem from love or deep feelings for others. Instead, it comes from having a balanced character and knowing how to interact well with people.

Truthfulness

Being honest is an important part of social life. Some people brag. They inflate their successes to look better than they are. Some people downplay their abilities—they pretend they are less skilled than they really are.

The best person is honest about themselves. They don't exaggerate or downplay who they are. Some people lie just for fun. Others lie to gain money or fame.

A boaster who lies to seem important is not as bad as someone who lies to trick others for money, but both are dishonest. People who act too humble may seem polite, but if they always pretend to be less than they are, it can seem fake.

The most honest person tells the truth in a fair and respectful way. If they do understate their abilities, they do so out of respect for others, not to deceive.

Sense of Humor and Tact

Life isn't just about serious matters—having fun and knowing how to joke is important too. But like everything else, there needs to be a balance.

Some people joke too much, often in ways that are rude or hurtful. Others never joke at all and take everything too seriously. The best person finds the middle ground.

A well-balanced person:

- Knows how to joke in a way that is fun but respectful.
- Enjoys humor without being offensive.
- Understands the right time and place for making jokes.

People who joke too much and don't care if they offend others are called buffoons. People who never joke and don't enjoy humor at all are seen as boring or dull.

A person with a good sense of humor makes social situations fun. They can lighten the mood without being rude or inappropriate.

The Importance of Balance in Social Life

Friendliness, truthfulness, and humor are vital traits in how we connect with others.

- Friendliness is about being kind but not fake.
- Truthfulness is about being honest but not boastful.
- A good sense of humor makes life fun, but it should never be used to hurt others.

In all social situations, the best person is the one who finds the right balance—not too much and not too little of each virtue.

A Quasi-Virtue - Shame

Shame is not a true virtue—it is an emotion, like fear. People feel shame when they fear losing respect, just as they feel fear when facing danger. Since it is a reaction, not a character trait, it is closer to an instinct than a moral quality.

Shame is most common in the young, who are more prone to mistakes. It helps them learn and avoid wrongdoing, which is why we see it as useful for youth. However, in adults, we expect right action to come from wisdom, not fear of embarrassment.

A truly good person doesn't need shame—they do what's right regardless of who is watching. Some think that feeling ashamed shows good character. But this idea is wrong. If someone is truly virtuous, they wouldn't act shamefully at all.

While shame can discourage bad behavior, it is not a virtue. Just because shamelessness is bad does not mean shame itself is good. It is simply a response to wrongdoing, not a quality that makes someone better.

Reflection & Application: Virtues of Wealth, Honor, and Social Life

Reflection Questions

- Generosity isn't about how much you give, but how

you give. Do you manage your resources in a way that allows you to be generous?

• Have you ever seen wastefulness disguised as generosity? What's the difference between truly helping others and spending just to impress people?

• Pride is about knowing your worth. Do you sometimes downplay your skills? Do you hesitate to accept praise you deserve? Or do you sometimes seek more praise than you deserve?

• How do you handle anger? Do you tend to overreact, or do you avoid confrontation even when you should speak up?

• When was the last time someone's sense of humor made a situation better? What makes humor effective rather than harmful?

• Do you do the right thing because it's right, or because you fear shame or judgment? How can you develop character that isn't dependent on outside approval?

Actionable Steps

✓ Give generously, but wisely. Look for meaningful ways to help others within your means. True generosity isn't about impressing people—it's about impact.

✓ Stand in your worth. If you deserve recognition, accept it gracefully. If you tend to seek too much praise, focus on letting your actions speak for themselves.

✓ Find balance in ambition. Don't avoid honor when you deserve it, but don't chase it at any cost. Work toward meaningful success.

✓ Control anger, don't suppress it. Speak up when necessary, but avoid holding grudges or lashing out impulsively.

✓ Use humor well. Lighten the mood without offending. A well-timed joke can ease tension, but an insensitive one can harm relationships.

✓ Do what's right, even without an audience. Instead of acting out of fear of shame, build habits that make integrity second nature.

5

JUSTICE

Justice: Its Meaning and Importance

J ustice is the foundation of fairness and ethical action. To fully understand it, we must explore:

What justice applies to—the actions and decisions it governs.

• Fairness is about justice. It helps create balance in various situations.

• How justice avoids extremes—finding the middle ground between too much and too little.

Most people think of justice as a quality that makes someone act fairly and want fairness for others. Injustice, on the other hand, is when someone acts unfairly or wants unfair things.

A just person always chooses fair actions, just as a healthy person makes choices that keep them well. Unlike skills or knowledge, which can be used for both good and bad, justice only leads to good actions.

There are two main types of justice:

1 Universal Justice – Doing what is right for society by following the law.
2 Particular Justice means being fair in specific cases. This could mean helping each other out or fixing issues when someone is treated unfairly.

Both types are important, but they focus on different things.

Universal Justice: Following the Law and Doing What's Right

A just person follows the law. They do this not just to obey but because laws bring order. This order helps people live together in peace. Good laws help shape citizens. They encourage virtues such as courage, honesty, and kindness.

For example, laws:

- Tell soldiers not to run away from battle.
- Tell people not to steal or cheat.
- Encourage fair and respectful behavior.

A well-made law helps people become good, while a poorly made law may not be as effective.

Many believe universal justice is the greatest virtue. It includes all virtues, like courage and kindness. A just person doesn't only think of themselves. They treat others fairly. Justice is one of the most important qualities in society.

Some people may be good in their personal lives but fail to treat others fairly. Justice ensures that a person is not only good individually but also fair to others.

Particular Justice: Fairness in Everyday Life

Universal justice rules laws and society. Particular justice focuses on making sure that people treat each other fairly. It applies in two key areas:

1 Distributive Justice – Sharing things like money, rewards, or honors in a fair way.
2 Rectificatory Justice – Making things right when someone is treated unfairly.

There are two types of wrongful actions that rectificatory justice deals with:

• Voluntary wrongs – When two people make an agreement (like trading or borrowing), but one person is unfair.
• Involuntary wrongs are crimes that harm others

without their consent. Examples include theft, cheating, and physical harm.

Justice restores fairness in both cases.

Why Justice Matters

Justice is not just about being a good person—it is the foundation of a fair society.

- Universal justice ensures that laws help everyone live together in peace.
- Particular justice ensures fairness in specific situations.

When people practice justice, they build a world. In this world, fairness, respect, and equality lead our actions.

Distributive Justice: Fair Sharing Based on Merit

Justice is about fairness, but what does that really mean? Many people believe justice means equality, but that's not always the case.

Justice is about fair balance, not just equality. It ensures that people receive what they truly deserve, based on their contributions. If two people differ in merit, treating them the same may actually be unfair.

Problems arise when:

- Equals are treated unequally.
- Unequals are treated the same.

This is where distributive justice comes in. It ensures that rewards are given fairly based on what people contribute.

Different groups define merit in different ways:

- Democrats believe merit means being a free citizen.
- Oligarchs believe it means being wealthy or noble.
- Aristocrats believe it means having virtue.

In justice, fairness is about balance. People get rewards based on what they've contributed. This is called geometrical proportion. It means the ratio of people matches the ratio of what they receive.

If this proportion is not followed, unfairness occurs. In good things (like wealth or success), an unjust person takes more than their share, while another gets too little. In tough times, like punishments or losses, the unfair person escapes their share. Meanwhile, someone else suffers more than necessary.

Justice uses this system to share wealth, honors, and privileges fairly.

Rectificatory Justice: Fixing Unfairness

The second type of justice is rectificatory justice, which is about fairness in dealing with others. It applies to two main areas:

1 Voluntary transactions mean fairness in trade, loans, and contracts.

2 Involuntary wrongs – Fixing theft, fraud, or harm done to others.

Rectificatory justice corrects injustices and restores fairness. Rectificatory justice differs from distributive justice. Distributive justice allocates resources based on merit. In contrast, rectificatory justice aims to correct wrongs. It does this without regard for wealth, status, or background. The goal is simple: to restore balance and make things right.

For example, if someone steals money or hurts another person, the law doesn't care about their status or background. It only looks at the unfair action and tries to fix it by making the wrongdoer repay or be punished.

A judge's job is to correct unfairness. If one person gains unfairly and another loses unfairly, the judge must take away the unfair gain and return it to the person who was wronged.

This way, both sides end up with what rightfully belongs to them.

The concept of "gain and loss" started with trade. If someone takes more than their fair share, they gain unfairly. Meanwhile, someone who gets too little is cheated. But this idea applies to all kinds of unfair situations—whether in business, crime, or personal disputes.

Justice is about restoring balance so that no one has too much or too little of what is fair.

Justice in Exchange and Fair Trade

Some people believe that justice is about giving back what you receive. The ancient Pythagoreans even said:

"A person should suffer the same as what they did to others."

This idea sounds fair, but it doesn't always work. For example, if a government leader hurts someone, it may not be fair to simply hurt them back. If someone attacks a leader, they might deserve a harsher punishment than just being attacked in return. Accidents are different from deliberate actions and should not be punished the same way.

"Eye for an eye" justice may not be fair, but fairness in trade and exchange is essential for society to work. People expect to give and receive fairly—otherwise, they feel cheated.

To make fair exchanges, proportional trade is needed. For example, a builder and a shoemaker both make useful things, but a house is worth much more than a pair of shoes. A shoemaker cannot trade a single pair of shoes for a house —such an exchange would be unbalanced. Instead, they must offer something of equal value, like many pairs of shoes or another service, to ensure fairness.

Because different things have different values, money was created to help with fair trade. Money allows people to measure value and make sure exchanges are balanced.

If people don't follow fair trade, society breaks down. Without fair exchanges, people wouldn't be able to trust each other or work together.

Justice as Balance

Justice is about finding the middle ground between having too much and too little. An unjust person takes more than their fair share of good things and less than their fair share of burdens. A person treated unfairly gets too little of what they deserve and too much hardship.

Justice is unique among virtues because it is not just a personal trait—it is an active force that restores balance in society. A just person chooses to act fairly, while an unjust person takes more than they should and makes others suffer more.

Political Justice and Other Types of Justice

Not every unjust action means the person is truly unjust in character. Someone might steal out of desperation. A person might act unfairly because they were angry or afraid, not because they are truly bad.

Justice in a society is called political justice. It only exists among free and equal people who live under laws.

Laws are necessary because they:

- Create clear rules for fairness.
- Prevent rulers from abusing power.

A ruler is supposed to act fairly and not take more than they deserve. That's why laws exist—to keep those in power from becoming tyrants. A good leader protects justice and ensures fairness for all.

Justice in a family works differently. A father doesn't treat his child the same way he would another adult citizen. Household justice differs from political justice, but it also aims for fairness.

Natural vs. Legal Justice

Justice can be divided into two types:

1 Natural Justice – Rules that are always true, no matter where you live.
○ Example: Fire burns the same way in every country.
2 Legal Justice – Laws that are made by people and can change.
○ Example: Some countries set various punishments for crimes.

Some argue that all justice is based on human laws because laws change over time. However, this is only partly true.

While human laws can change, some basic rules of fairness never change.

For example, most people are born right-handed, but with training, a person can become skilled with both hands. Similarly, legal justice can change, but natural justice (basic fairness) stays the same.

Justice and Choice: Degrees of Wrongdoing

Justice depends on whether actions are done on purpose or by accident.

- If a person knowingly chooses to do something unfair, they are acting unjustly.
- If they do something unfair by accident, they are not truly unjust.

For example, if someone forces another person's hand to hit someone, that person isn't responsible. If someone accidentally hits their own father, they are still responsible. However, the situation influences how we see their actions.

Types of Wrongdoing

When people harm others, their actions usually fall into one of three categories:

1 Accidents (Misadventures) – These are harms that occur by chance and catch us off guard. They can't be predicted.

2 Mistakes – These happen when someone causes harm without meaning to, but their own poor judgment is to blame.

3 Acts of Injustice – These happen when someone knowingly and willingly causes harm, even if they act out of anger or emotion.

A person may harm someone out of strong emotions, like anger. They act unjustly in that moment, but it doesn't mean they are an unjust person overall. However, when someone chooses to harm another on purpose, they are truly unjust.

This is why we sometimes excuse actions done in anger —because the person who got angry may have been provoked. When someone plans to harm another, they must accept their responsibility.

Voluntary vs. Involuntary Actions

When judging fairness and justice, we must ask: Was the action intentional or accidental?

Some involuntary actions are excusable, like when someone makes a mistake due to ignorance. Other involuntary actions aren't excusable. This is true, especially when they stem from reckless emotions or bad habits.

Justice is about making fair choices. A just person acts fairly. An unjust person acts unfairly, especially when they break fairness or equality.

Can Someone Be Treated Unjustly Voluntarily?

Can a person choose to be treated unfairly? Now that we understand doing and suffering injustice, it's a good question to ask.

In a play by Euripides, a character asks:

"Were you both willing, or unwilling both?"

This raises a question: Is injustice always forced upon

someone, or can they accept it willingly? If committing injustice is a choice, does that mean suffering injustice is also a choice? Can someone be treated justly even when they don't want to be?

Not everyone who experiences something unfair is truly a victim of injustice. A person can cause harm by accident. A person can experience unfairness even if it isn't true injustice.

For example, if injustice only meant harm, then someone who gambles their money would be a victim. But this does not seem right. If a person lets others take advantage of them, it might be unfair, but is it truly injustice?

A well-known instance is in Homer's Iliad. A warrior named Glaucus swaps his golden armor for bronze armor. This trade is clearly unequal. However, since he willingly made the trade, he was not truly treated unjustly, even if the deal was unfair.

Injustice occurs only when someone chooses to act unjustly. Simply accepting an unfair situation does not always mean a person is a victim of injustice.

Who Is Responsible for Injustice in Distribution?

A key question is: When resources are shared unfairly, who is to blame? Is it the giver or the receiver?

This connects to another debate: Can a person treat themselves unfairly?

Is it unfair for someone to give away more than they keep for themselves? Virtuous people sometimes give up wealth or power for the sake of fairness, but does this mean they are victims of injustice?

The answer depends on how we define injustice. A person is only treated unjustly if they receive something against their will. When someone decides to give more to others, they aren't forced into an unfair situation. So, they aren't really a victim of injustice.

The real injustice happens when the person in charge unfairly divides resources on purpose. A person getting more isn't always unfair. They may not be taking advantage of an unjust system. If the distributor makes an honest mistake, they are not guilty of legal injustice. However, if they create unfairness on purpose—like giving land in exchange for a bribe—then they are acting unjustly.

Justice Is Harder Than It Seems

Many people believe that being just is easy, but that is not true.

Committing injustice (like lying or stealing) is easy.

Becoming an unjust person doesn't happen overnight. It takes time. You choose unfair actions again and again. Eventually, it becomes part of your character. Being truly just is more than following laws—it requires wisdom and fair judgment.

Some believe justice is simple because laws define right and wrong. Laws provide general rules, but real justice needs a grasp of each situation. For example, in medicine it is easy to know that honey, wine, and surgery can heal people. But knowing when, how, and for whom to use them is the skill of a true doctor. Similarly, justice is not just about knowing the law—it is about applying fairness wisely in real life.

Equity: When Laws Are Not Enough

Sometimes, laws are too rigid and do not fit every situation. This is where equity comes in.

- Laws use general terms. However, real-life situations can be too complex for a single law to cover everything.
- Equity allows justice to be more flexible, making sure the law is applied fairly in special cases.

Think of it like a measuring tool:

- A rigid ruler may not work well for shaping stone, because stone is uneven.
- A flexible ruler bends to fit the material and measure more accurately.

In the same way, equity allows laws to work as they were meant to, even when a strict legal rule would lead to an unfair result. A person who is truly just does not just follow the law blindly—they seek fairness for everyone involved.

Thus, equity is not separate from justice—it is a necessary part of true justice.

Can a Person Treat Themselves Unjustly?

Some people ask: Can a person be unjust to themselves?

1 Justice Requires More Than One Person

○ The law does not allow suicide, not because a person is unjust to themselves, but because it harms society.
○ Throughout history, governments punished suicide attempts. They viewed these acts as harm to the state.

2 Justice Requires an Active Doer and a Passive Receiver

○ A person cannot steal from themselves, because they already own what they take.
○ Adultery, theft, or burglary make no sense within one person.

3 If someone can treat themselves unfairly, they can also choose to be treated unfairly by others.

○ But we have already said no one can willingly suffer injustice—so the idea of self-injustice doesn't make sense.

Is It Worse to Act Unjustly or to Be Treated Unjustly?

Both are bad:

- To be treated unjustly means getting less than you deserve.
- To act unjustly means taking more than you deserve.

However, acting unjustly is worse because it is a choice and shows a deeper flaw in character.

At the same time, being treated unfairly can sometimes lead to greater harm in specific situations.

Justice is meant for people who live together and must share what is good. It is the virtue that keeps society fair and balanced.

Reflection & Application: Justice and Fairness

Reflection Questions

- When have you seen justice misunderstood as strict equality rather than fair balance? Can you think of a situation where treating two people exactly the same would actually be unfair?
- Have you ever had to correct an unfair situation?

Did you succeed in restoring balance, or did obstacles get in the way?

• What do you think is harder: creating fair laws for everyone or applying them fairly in specific cases? Why?

• In your daily life, do you lean more toward strict rules or flexible fairness? How do you decide when to follow rules exactly and when to adapt to the situation?

• Do you think people today value justice as much as other virtues like kindness or courage? Why or why not?

• Is suffering injustice always bad? Can it ever lead to personal growth or a better understanding of fairness?

Actionable Steps

✓ Seek fairness, not just equality. Think about whether treating everyone "the same" is really fair. Different situations might need different responses.

✓ Practice justice in small ways. Be fair at work, in friendships, and in daily choices. Share responsibilities, rewards, and punishments equally.

✓ Correct injustice when you see it. If you notice unfair treatment, speak up or take action to restore balance.

✓ Be mindful of biases in judgment. Justice means

being fair. So, it's important to keep personal feelings out of decisions.

✔ Respect laws, but think critically. Laws aim to create justice, but they sometimes need flexibility to ensure fairness in real life.

✔ Remember that fairness applies to both giving and receiving. Being fair doesn't just mean sharing with others—it also means accepting what you deserve.

6

INTELLECTUAL VIRTUE

Why Studying Intellectual Virtue Matters

Being virtuous means finding the right balance—not too much, not too little. This balance is called the "mean," and it's based on reason. But what does "correct reason" really mean? Telling someone to "Be reasonable" isn't useful. It's like saying, "Take the medicine the doctor prescribes," without saying which one. We need to understand what correct reasoning is and how to recognize it.

The soul contains two kinds of virtues. First, there are moral virtues, such as courage and self-control. Then, there are intellectual virtues, which aid in wise thinking. We've discussed moral virtues. Now, let's explore intellectual virtues. First, we need to understand how the mind works.

The Two Sides of Our Thinking

Our mind has two main ways of thinking:

1 Contemplative (Scientific) Thinking – Focuses on facts that never change.
2 Practical Thinking – Helps us make decisions about things that can change.

Each kind of thinking needs its own special virtue. Understanding these virtues helps us use our minds in the best way.

Thinking vs. Doing

Everything has a purpose, and the purpose of thinking is to find the truth. But different types of thinking do this in different ways:

• Scientific thinking looks for truth about things that are always the same.
• Practical thinking looks for truth that helps us make good choices.

Good decisions come from two things: clear thinking and good desires. Moral virtue helps us want the right things, while intellectual virtue helps us think correctly. Together, they lead to good choices.

But thinking alone doesn't make things happen—only

practical thinking leads to action. Even when we create things, we are aiming toward an end goal. But the highest goal isn't just making things—it's doing good actions.

That's why we say: *"A good choice is when reason and desire work together."*

Also, we can't choose things that have already happened —only things we can still control. As the poet Agathon said: *"Even the gods can't change the past."*

So while both types of thinking look for truth, they do it in different ways. Now, let's look at the key intellectual virtues.

The Five Intellectual Virtues

There are five main ways our mind finds truth:

1 Art (Techne) – Knowing how to make things.
2 Scientific Knowledge (Episteme) – Knowing facts that always stay the same.
3 Practical Wisdom (Phronesis) – Knowing how to make good choices.
4 Philosophic Wisdom (Sophia) – The deepest kind of wisdom.
5 Intuitive Reason (Nous) – The skill to grasp simple truths right away.

We don't include opinions because they can be wrong. Real intellectual virtues must lead to the truth.

What Is Scientific Knowledge?

Scientific knowledge is about facts that never change. That's what makes it different from opinions, which can be wrong or change over time.

Because science is based on facts, it is permanent and unchanging. It must also be something we can learn and teach, which happens in two ways:

- Induction – Looking at examples and figuring out general rules.
- Deduction – Using general rules to make conclusions.

Both are important. We start by observing things (induction) and then use general rules to think logically (deduction).

So, scientific knowledge can be defined as: *"A way of thinking that helps us understand and explain the truth."*

Art – Knowing How to Make Things

There are two types of skills we use in life:

1 Creating – This means building houses, painting art, or making tools.
2 Doing – This involves making decisions, solving problems, and taking action.

These are different skills, so the knowledge needed for each is also different.

Art (techne) is the kind of knowledge that helps us create things. For example, architecture is an art because it involves planning and building.

Art is about knowing how to make something that does not occur naturally—it requires human creativity and skill. A house, a painting, or a sculpture would never exist on their own; they must be crafted through deliberate effort.

That's why art is different from other types of knowledge —it is about creating things, not just understanding them. As the poet Agathon said:

"Art loves chance, and chance loves art."

This means that creativity and luck sometimes work together.

Practical Wisdom – Knowing How to Make Good Life Decisions

Practical wisdom (phronesis) helps people make smart choices in life.

A wise person knows how to make good decisions for themselves and others. This isn't just about one specific area (like health or strength), but about living well overall.

Practical wisdom differs from science. Science is about facts. Practical wisdom considers the circumstances.

How is practical wisdom different from art?

- Art is about producing something external—like a

painting, a house, or a sculpture. Its value comes from the finished product.

• Practical wisdom is about acting wisely in real-life situations. A good action is valuable in itself, not because it creates something tangible.

Leaders like Pericles, who was from Athens, were seen as wise. They knew what was good for themselves and what benefited the whole community.

Practical wisdom also requires self-control (sophrosyne). People ruled by pleasure or pain can lose sight of what truly matters. If someone lets emotions take over, they forget why they made a decision in the first place.

Practical wisdom differs from art. In art, a skilled person can make deliberate mistakes. But in practical wisdom, a truly wise person would never choose poorly on purpose.

Intuitive Reason – Instantly Recognizing Truths

Scientific knowledge helps us understand what is always true. But science needs a foundation—it must start from basic truths that cannot be proven by science itself.

These first principles—the foundation of all knowledge —cannot come from:

• Science – Science relies on logic to prove facts, but it must begin with basic truths that cannot be proven.
• Art or practical wisdom deals with things that change. First principles are truths that do not change.

So, how do we know these first truths? We understand them through intuitive reason (nous). This means we can quickly recognize basic truths without needing proof.

Philosophic Wisdom – The Deepest Knowledge

The word wisdom (sophia) can mean different things. A person can be wise in a specific skill (like a wise sculptor) or a person can be wise in a general sense (someone who deeply understands the world).

Philosophic wisdom is the highest kind of wisdom because it combines:

1 Scientific knowledge – Knowing universal truths.
2 Intuitive reason – Understanding first principles.

Some people think politics is the highest knowledge, but this is not true. Humans are not the most important things in the universe—there are greater things, like the stars and the heavens.

Philosophic wisdom aims to grasp the biggest, most important truths.

Anaxagoras and Thales were called wise. This wasn't due to practicality. Instead, they grasped deep, complex truths about the universe.

However, philosophic wisdom is not the same as practical wisdom.

• Philosophic wisdom seeks knowledge for its own sake.
• Practical wisdom helps us make good choices in life.

Practical Wisdom vs. Theoretical Wisdom

• Practical wisdom is about human actions and choices—things we can change by deciding to act.
• Theoretical wisdom focuses on understanding unchanging truths.

For example, a wise person does not just understand general ideas like *"healthy food is good for you."* They also know the details, like *"chicken is healthy."* This is why experienced people often make better decisions than those who only have book knowledge.

Practical wisdom focuses on real-life actions. So, it is one of the key intellectual virtues.

Practical Wisdom and Political Science

Practical wisdom helps us make good life choices. Political wisdom guides community governance. They are linked, but they are not the same.

There are two types of political wisdom:

1 Legislative wisdom – Creating laws and setting rules for a community.

2 Political wisdom – Using laws to make fair decisions for the people.

Practical wisdom is also used in other areas of life:

• Household management – Running a home and family wisely.
• Legislation – Creating fair and effective laws.
• Political leadership – Choosing what's best for everyone in the community.
• Judicial Wisdom – Grasping Fairness and Justice in Court Rulings.

Some believe the smartest thing is to only care about yourself. They see politicians as people who interfere too much in others' lives.

But others argue that no one can truly live well without a functioning society. Managing personal life wisely is connected to managing a community wisely.

Wisdom Comes With Experience

Practical wisdom is not something you can learn from books alone—it comes with experience. A young person might be good at math or science, but they lack wisdom about life. Young people can easily learn geometry. But they often find philosophy and politics harder. This is because those subjects need a grasp of people and real-life experiences.

What Makes Someone Good at Decision-Making?

Good decision-making isn't just about thinking. It's about working through a problem carefully to find the best solution. Good decisions are different from science. Science seeks fixed truths, but decisions must adapt to changing situations. It is not the same as guessing, because good decisions require time and thought, while guesses are often quick and random.

There are different kinds of correct thinking, but not all of them lead to wise decisions:

- A clever but selfish person might plan something harmful very well. Even though their thinking is correct, they are not using wisdom for good.
- A person might make the right choice but for the wrong reasons. This is still not true wisdom.
- Someone might think too long about a simple choice. True wisdom is about knowing the right thing to do, at the right time, in the right way.

Good decision-making means thinking about the best way to reach a good goal. People with practical wisdom make great decisions. They know what is good for themselves and for others.

Understanding vs. Practical Wisdom

Understanding, or synesis, is a key type of thinking. It is different from practical wisdom because it does not involve making decisions or taking action. Instead, it helps people judge situations correctly.

For example:

• Someone with practical wisdom knows what should be done.
• A person who understands can tell if something makes sense.

Understanding helps us listen to others better. A person with understanding can tell if an idea is reasonable or unrealistic.

This is why people who understand ideas are often seen as wise, even if they aren't the ones making decisions.

Judgment and Fairness

Some people have good judgment—they can recognize what is fair and reasonable.

When we call someone a fair judge, we mean they are good at deciding what is right in a situation.

Good judgment is important because it helps us understand truth and fairness. It links to other traits like understanding, practical wisdom, and intuition. These qualities help people make better decisions.

Smart decision-makers use their experience and think carefully. Some think wisdom is just for big ideas. But real wisdom is also about solving everyday problems.

Older people, or those with more life experience, often have better judgment. They have seen and learned from many situations, so they recognize what is fair and what is not. That's why we should listen to wise and experienced people, just as much as we listen to logical arguments.

What Is the Purpose of Wisdom?

Some people ask: Why do we need wisdom?

- Philosophical wisdom sheds light on big ideas. However, it may not aid in making practical decisions.
- If practical wisdom helps us make good choices, does a naturally good person still need it? Can someone be truly virtuous without wisdom to guide their actions?
- Why does practical wisdom seem more important in daily life if philosophy is greater?

The answer is simple: Both types of wisdom are important.

- Practical wisdom helps us not just understand what is good, but actually do good things.
- Wisdom is about living rightly, not just knowing what is right.

For example, being healthy isn't about knowing facts about health—it's about actually being in good health.

In the same way, being wise isn't about knowing what is right, but actually acting wisely.

The Connection Between Wisdom and Virtue

Being wise isn't just about thinking well—it's about being good. Cleverness helps people reach their goals, but if their goals are selfish or harmful, this isn't true wisdom. Practical wisdom is different because it aims at what is truly good.

Some people are naturally brave, kind, or fair, but without wisdom, they might use these qualities in the wrong way.

For example:

- A strong person without sight might stumble and fall.
- A good person without wisdom might make bad decisions.

Socrates, the philosopher, believed that virtues like kindness and bravery are forms of wisdom. But he wasn't completely right—virtues aren't just knowledge; they must be used wisely.

This is why:

- A person cannot be truly good without wisdom.
- A person cannot be truly wise without goodness.

They go hand in hand.

Is Practical Wisdom More Important Than Philosophy?

Even though practical wisdom helps us act, it doesn't rule over philosophical wisdom.

Think of it like this. A doctor helps people become healthy, but health itself is more important than medicine. Practical wisdom helps us act well, but the highest wisdom is about understanding the deeper meaning of life.

Saying practical wisdom is more important than philosophy would be like saying a political leader is greater than the gods just because they make decisions for people. That would be a mistake.

Both practical wisdom and philosophical wisdom hold great value. Practical wisdom helps us make good choices. Philosophical wisdom shows us the deeper truths of life.

Reflection & Application: The Role of Wisdom in a Good Life

Reflection Questions

- Do you value knowing things, like philosophical wisdom, or making good choices, like practical wisdom? Why?
- Have you ever made a mistake because you lacked practical wisdom (even though you had knowledge)? What did you learn from that experience?

• How do you balance logic and experience when making a decision? Do you rely more on facts, intuition, or past experiences?

• Can someone be too wise in one area but lack wisdom in another? (For example, a brilliant scientist who makes bad personal decisions.) How can we develop wisdom in all areas of life?

• How can young people gain wisdom if it comes from experience? They haven't lived through many situations yet.

• Is it better to focus on practical wisdom for daily life or philosophic wisdom for finding life's purpose? Or do we need both equally?

Actionable Steps

✓ Improve your practical wisdom by reflecting on past choices. What decisions worked well? What would you do differently next time?

✓ Seek out experienced mentors. Wisdom comes from experience, so learning from those who have lived through challenges can help you grow.

✓ Practice making thoughtful decisions. Before acting, ask: Is this choice guided by logic, experience, and moral goodness?

✓ Balance knowledge with action. Don't just collect information—use what you learn to improve your life and help others.

✓ Develop both types of wisdom. Learn about big

ideas (philosophy) but also focus on daily decision-making (practical wisdom).

7

SELF-CONTROL AND LACK OF SELF-CONTROL—PLEASURE

Different Types of Character: How We Should Understand Them

There are three types of bad moral character:

- ○ Vice: being morally bad.
- ○ Lack of self-control: not being able to manage one's impulses.
- ○ Brutishness: acting like an animal.

The opposite of vice is virtue, and the opposite of lack of self-control is self-control. Brutishness is not good at all. It contrasts with regular virtue and what some refer to as "superhuman virtue" or "heroic goodness."

Some people believe that if a person becomes extremely good, they almost become like a god. If that's true, then this godlike virtue would be the opposite of brutishness. Just as animals don't have moral values (they aren't truly good or bad), neither do gods—they are beyond human virtues and vices.

Now, godlike people are rare, just like brutish people are rare. The Spartans, when they admired someone greatly, called them "godlike." Brutish people can often be seen in certain groups, such as some barbarian tribes. However, some individuals may become brutish due to illness or deformity. We also call extremely wicked people "brutish." We'll discuss that later. For now, let's turn our attention to self-control, lack of self-control, and endurance. These traits are not just good or bad. They are complex and deserve to be looked at individually.

As always, we should first lay out the facts as they appear, then work through any difficulties in understanding them. Our goal is to prove, as much as possible, that the common ideas people have about these qualities are true. We may not prove everything, but we should prove the most reasonable ones. These are the ones backed by respected opinions. If we can explain things clearly and respect common beliefs, we will have done our job well.

Now, people generally think:

1 Self-control and endurance are good traits. They are admirable. On the other hand, a lack of self-control and weakness are bad. They bring shame.
2 A person with self-control listens to reason. But

someone without it lets emotions take over, even if they know it's not right.

3 A temperate person is seen as having self-control. But not everyone believes that all self-controlled people are temperate. Some people confuse lack of self-control with indulgence. They think giving in to pleasures is the same. But others believe these are different.

4 Some believe a wise person cannot lack self-control, while others think some wise people do struggle with it.

5 People can lack self-control in more than just pleasure—they can struggle with anger, ambition, or greed as well.

Questioning These Ideas

Now, we need to ask: What kind of thinking does a person have when they act without self-control? Some say it's impossible for someone to do something they know is wrong. Socrates, for example, argued that people only do bad things because they misunderstand what is truly good. He thought that if someone truly knew what was right, they would follow it. This would mean self-control wasn't needed.

But this idea doesn't match what we actually see in real life. So, we need to figure out what happens when someone lacks self-control. If they are acting out of ignorance, what kind of ignorance is it? We know that before someone gives in to temptation, they don't believe they should act that way.

Some people partly agree with Socrates. They think knowledge is strong. But they see that people can overlook their better judgment. They argue that when someone loses self-control, they don't have real knowledge—just an opinion. If it's just a weak opinion, then we might understand why it doesn't stand up to strong desires. We don't blame people for weak convictions, but we do blame them for being wicked.

What Does Self-Control Really Mean?

Does self-control mean resisting bad desires? If so, does a self-controlled person need to have strong bad desires? A balanced and moderate person wouldn't be seen as self-controlled. They wouldn't have strong desires to resist. On the other hand, if someone resists good desires, then their self-control wouldn't be admirable. And if their desires are weak and bad, resisting them wouldn't be impressive either.

Is Self-Control Always Good?

Another question: Is self-control always good? If someone stubbornly holds onto a false belief, that's bad. If a lack of self-control means giving up beliefs, it can be good sometimes. Look at Neoptolemus in Sophocles' Philoctetes, for instance. He gave up on telling a lie, even though Odysseus had convinced him it was necessary, because he felt bad about lying.

Some find this tricky: If a person has poor self-control

and goes against their beliefs, they might view something bad as good. In that case, they will end up doing what is actually good! That would mean a foolish and impulsive person could end up acting virtuously by accident, which seems absurd.

Who Truly Lacks Self-Control?

One last problem: Is a person who knowingly chooses pleasure worse than someone who gives in to pleasure out of weakness? Some say the first person is worse because they at least believe in what they're doing, so they can be convinced to change their mind. But someone without self-control ignores even what they believe, so how can you reason with them? That's where the saying comes in: *"When water chokes you, what can you wash it down with?"*—meaning, if reasoning doesn't work, what else can you use?

In the end, if self-control can relate to everything, who really lacks self-control overall? Some people struggle with self-control more than others.

How Can an Incontinent Person Know Something Is Wrong but Still Do It?

Many people have a hard time with self-control. They know they should say no to some temptations, but it's tough. To understand why, we need to explore a few key questions:

- Does a person who lacks self-control (an incontinent person) act knowingly, or not? If they do know, what kind of knowledge do they have?

• What kinds of things do self-controlled and uncontrolled people struggle with? Are they affected by all kinds of pleasures and pains, or just certain ones?

• Are self-control and endurance the same thing, or different?

To begin, we need to figure out whether an incontinent person is defined by the type of desires they have, by how they react to them, or by both. We also need to ask whether self-control and lack of self-control apply to all kinds of temptations or just specific ones.

Someone without self-control isn't tempted by everything. They are attracted to the same pleasures as someone who indulges freely. However, there's a key difference:

• A self-indulgent person seeks pleasure intentionally. They think it's important to always pursue enjoyment.
• An incontinent person, on the other hand, knows they shouldn't give in but still does it anyway.

Does an Incontinent Person Have Knowledge or Just an Opinion?

Some say that a person with incontinence acts against what they think, not against what they truly know. But that doesn't change much. People often hold their opinions as firmly as others hold facts.

The word "know" can mean two different things:

- A person has knowledge but isn't actively thinking about it.
- A person has knowledge and is fully aware of it in the moment.

This difference matters. If a person does something wrong even while actively thinking about what they know, that seems strange. But if they act wrongly because they aren't thinking about their knowledge at that moment, it makes more sense.

How Can Someone Know Something but Still Ignore It?

When making decisions, people combine two types of knowledge:

- General truths—Big ideas that apply to everyone. (Example: "Eating healthy food is good for people.")
- Specific facts—Personal facts about themselves. (Example: "I am a person.")

Put together, these ideas form a conclusion: "Eating healthy food is good for me."

When someone loses self-control, they may recall the general truth. But they might not apply it to their specific situation. They might know sweets are unhealthy in general but not stop to think, *"This cookie is unhealthy for me right now."* If they don't connect the general idea to their specific choice, they might give in to temptation.

Also, knowledge can exist in different states. Sometimes, people *have* knowledge but aren't thinking about it clearly. This can happen when they are:

- Asleep
- Drunk
- Overcome by emotions (like anger or strong desire)

In these cases, people might share things they've heard, like facts or rules. But they don't really understand or control what they do at that time. The same happens when someone loses self-control: they *know* what's right but don't *act* on it.

How Passion Overpowers Reason

When making decisions, people mix two kinds of thoughts:

- General knowledge (big ideas)
- Immediate, real-world facts (what's happening right now)

For example:

- *"Everything sweet should be tasted."* (A general belief)
- *"This is sweet."* (A specific fact)

If nothing holds them back, they'll follow through and eat the sweet thing. But here's the problem. If they also believe, *"Sweets aren't healthy, so I shouldn't eat them,"* their emotions (like desire) might override this belief.

A person may know they shouldn't eat sweets. But their feelings can lead them to choose otherwise.

This also explains why animals can't lose self-control the way humans do. Animals don't think in general ideas—they only react to what they see and remember. Since they don't reason like humans, they don't struggle with self-control the way we do.

How Do People Regain Self-Control?

Regaining self-control is like how a drunk person sobers up or how someone wakes from sleep. Their reasoning comes back.

Someone feeling strong emotions may say something wise, but they often don't grasp it or act on it right away. It's similar to how a drunk person can repeat wise words yet fail to act wisely.

So, Socrates was partly right: when people lose self-control, they aren't acting with full knowledge. But let's adds an important idea: it's not that they *lack* knowledge—it's that their emotions stop them from using it properly.

This explains how a person can know what's right and still act against it.

What Does It Mean to Lack Self-Control?

Now, we need to ask: Is there such a thing as a person who lacks self-control in every way, or are people only incontinent in specific areas?

People with self-control and those without both have a hard time with pleasure and pain. But not all pleasures are the same. Some are necessary, like food and sleep, while others—such as wealth, fame, and winning—are desirable but not essential.

This difference is important:

- A person who loses control over money, honor, or anger isn't simply called "incontinent." Instead, we say they are incontinent about *money* or *anger.* These people resemble those who lack self-control, but they aren't quite the same.
- True incontinence relates to bodily pleasures. It includes overeating, drinking too much, and avoiding discomfort at all costs. Losing control over food or comfort is seen as a major weakness. But losing control over wealth or ambition doesn't carry the same shame.
- We group incontinent people with self-indulgent ones. Self-indulgent people fully give in to pleasure. But there's a key difference:
  ○ A self-indulgent person chooses to overindulge. They think pleasure is the best thing in life.

○ An incontinent person knows they should resist but still fails to do so.

This also explains why someone who chases pleasure without even having a strong craving is even worse. If they can't resist *mild* temptation, what would they do if they had a really intense desire?

Not All Desires Are Bad

Not all pleasures are dangerous. Some, like success, honor, or love for family, are naturally good things to want. People aren't blamed for simply having these desires, but they are blamed when their desires go too far.

For example, myths tell of people whose love for their families became excessive. Niobe was so proud of her children that she refused to honor the gods, which led to her downfall. Satyrus was so devoted to his father that people thought he was foolish. These people weren't bad, but their desires became extreme.

Because things like honor and family love are naturally good, going too far with them isn't wicked—it's just excessive. This is why true incontinence (lack of self-control) doesn't apply to them. When people lose control over ambition or wealth, we might liken them to those who lack self-control. However, this isn't the same as losing control over physical pleasures like food and comfort.

Extreme Cases: Brutish and Morbid Incontinence

Not all desires come from natural human urges. Some come from habits, illness, or something deeply unnatural.

• Some people develop strange cravings, like eating dirt or chewing their nails.
• Others act in ways that seem inhuman, either because of mental illness or because they were raised in a brutal way.
• Certain tribes were said to eat raw meat or even human flesh. Some people, in moments of madness, even harmed their own family members.

These behaviors don't come from normal human desires but from something far more extreme. A person like this isn't just incontinent. Their issue goes beyond temptation. It often relates to a deeper problem, such as an illness or an unnatural habit.

We wouldn't label a sick person as incontinent just for acting strangely. Also, we wouldn't say someone is incontinent just because of a harsh upbringing. A tyrant like Phalaris might have felt the urge to eat human flesh but stopped himself. If someone can't control themselves, their issue isn't just incontinence. It's something much more serious.

This is similar to how we separate different types of wickedness. Normal wickedness stems from poor choices. Brutish wickedness comes from deeper problems. These include an animal-like nature or mental illness. We should separate normal incontinence from brutish or disease-driven behavior. Normal incontinence is about struggling with bodily pleasures. Brutish behavior is quite different.

Why Losing Control of Anger Is Less Shameful Than Losing Control of Desires

Now, let's compare losing control over anger to losing control over pleasures like food and comfort. Which is worse?

1 Anger follows reason—just not very well. It reacts first and thinks later, like a dog barking at a noise before realizing it's just the wind. Desire, on the other hand, ignores reason completely. It doesn't just bark —it runs straight for what it wants, no questions asked.

2 People tend to forgive natural impulses more easily. Everyone gets angry, but excessive desire isn't as natural. Stories say that sons hit their fathers because the fathers hit their grandfathers. Anger runs in families and is seen as part of human nature, while uncontrolled desire is not.

3 Angry people act in the moment, while pleasure-seekers are sneaky. An angry person lashes out immediately, but those ruled by desire often plot and scheme to get what they want. Poets describe love and desire as "tricky" and "cunning," making them seem worse than anger.

4 People who act out of anger feel pain, while those who act out of desire feel pleasure. No one commits a crime out of anger for fun, but people who chase pleasure often do. Crimes done for pleasure are worse than those done from pain. So, incontinence from appetite is more disgraceful than from anger.

This is why losing control over pleasure is worse than losing control over anger. Self-control and lack of self-control are mainly about bodily pleasures, but not all pleasures are the same. Some are normal and natural, while others are extreme or even unnatural.

Two Types of Incontinence: Weakness and Impulsiveness

Some people give in to temptation because they love pleasure. Others do it because they want to avoid pain. Both types struggle with self-control, but they are different.

- Weakness – This person knows what's right but hesitates. They think about resisting, but in the end, they give in.
- Impulsiveness – This person doesn't even stop to think. They follow their desires right away. They don't think about the consequences.

Between these two, weakness is seen as less shameful. A weak person at least tries to resist, while an impulsive person doesn't even pause to consider their actions.

A truly soft person struggles with pains that most people can handle. For example, some people avoid even small discomforts, like refusing to lift their own cloak. Others pretend to be sick, even when they aren't. Kings in some places were known for being weak and avoiding even the slightest hardship.

In general, people are judged more harshly if they give in to small temptations. If a person does something bad with only a weak urge, what would they do if their urges were strong? Self-indulgent people are seen as worse than incontinent ones. Self-indulgent folks choose to give in, but incontinent people at least fight their urges.

The opposite of an incontinent person is a continent person, who resists pleasure. The opposite of a soft person is a person of endurance, someone who withstands pain. These are different:

- Continent people win the battle against pleasure.
- People of endurance don't let pain defeat them.

Winning is harder than just not losing, which is why continence is more admirable than endurance.

People who love amusement and play too much aren't truly self-indulgent, but they are soft. Fun is supposed to be a break from work, not the main focus of life. Those who always seek fun and relaxation go too far with something that should only be enjoyed in moderation.

Impulsiveness vs. Weakness

There are two types of incontinence:

1 Impulsiveness – Acting without thinking, driven by emotions.
2 Weakness – Thinking things through but failing to follow through.

Some people lose control because they don't stop to think. They react right away. They follow their feelings, not their thoughts. Others think carefully but still fail to resist temptation when the moment arrives.

A person who knows they are ticklish can prepare themselves not to laugh. In the same way, someone who understands their weaknesses can plan ahead to resist temptation. But impulsive people don't wait for reason to catch up—they act on whatever seems right in the moment, whether it actually is or not.

Why Self-Indulgence Is Worse Than Incontinence

A self-indulgent person doesn't regret their choices. They believe chasing pleasure is the right thing to do. An incontinent person, on the other hand, knows they're doing something wrong but struggles to stop.

This is why self-indulgence is worse than incontinence:

• A self-indulgent person is incurable because they don't see a problem with their behavior.

• An incontinent person can be helped because they recognize their mistakes.

Self-indulgence is like a chronic disease, similar to a serious illness. Incontinence is more like epilepsy, with episodes that come and go.

There's another key difference:

• Self-indulgent people are unaware of their flaws.

• Incontinent people know they are wrong but still give in.

Sometimes, acting on impulse can lead to better results than careful thinking that ends in the wrong choice.

Virtue and vice depend on a person's core beliefs. Just as math is based on unproven first principles, a person's character is shaped by their basic values. Good people follow the right principles. Bad people choose the wrong ones.

A self-indulgent person is bad because their principles are flawed. They think pleasure is the highest good. An incontinent person, however, still has good principles; they just struggle to follow them. That's why incontinence, though bad, is not as bad as self-indulgence.

Continence, Incontinence, Stubbornness, and Temperance

Does self-control mean sticking to any belief, or only the right ones? Is incontinence just failing to stick to a decision, or failing to follow good reasoning?

The answer:

- A continent person follows the right reasoning.
- An incontinent person does not.

Some people look self-controlled when they won't change their minds. But really, they are just stubborn, not self-controlled.

Stubborn people include:

- Opinionated people – They refuse to accept new ideas.
- Ignorant people – They don't know they're wrong.
- Boors – They are too narrow-minded to consider other views.

These people resist change, but not for good reasons. A self-controlled person resists temptation for good reasons. A stubborn person, however, fights change even when logic tells them to adapt.

Not every failure to follow a decision is bad. For example, in Sophocles' play *Philoctetes*, Neoptolemus agrees to lie but later regrets it and tells the truth. He doesn't keep his promise to lie, but he breaks it for a noble reason—because truthfulness is good. This shows that not all changes in behavior are due to incontinence—only those caused by disgraceful desires.

There's also the issue of excessive avoidance of pleasure. Some people don't enjoy bodily pleasures as much as they should and don't follow reason either.

- The self-controlled person finds a healthy balance —they neither enjoy pleasure too much nor avoid it too much.
- Since self-control is good, both extremes—too much indulgence and too much avoidance—must be bad.
- Most people rarely avoid pleasure. Instead, they focus on the fight between self-control and indulgence.

The word "self-control" is often used loosely.

- A self-controlled person and a temperate person both resist pleasure, but they aren't the same. The temperate person doesn't want too much pleasure. The self-controlled person might want it, but they don't give in.
- An incontinent person and a self-indulgent person both seek pleasure. The self-indulgent person believes they should act this way, but the incontinent person does not.

Practical Wisdom vs. Cleverness in the Incontinent Person

A truly wise person cannot be incontinent. Wisdom requires both knowledge and good character. An incontinent person acts against their better judgment. So, they struggle to use wisdom properly.

However, an incontinent person can be clever.

Cleverness is the ability to think quickly and find solutions, but it is not the same as wisdom. Some people seem wise because they are clever, but in reality, they lack true wisdom because they can't control their desires.

An incontinent person is like someone who is asleep or drunk. They may know the truth inside, but they aren't fully aware of it at that moment.

Even though an incontinent person chooses to act wrongly, they aren't completely wicked. Their overall intentions are still good; they just fail to follow through. This makes them "half-wicked." They aren't criminals because they don't plan evil acts in advance.

There are two types of incontinent people:

1 Those who deliberate but fail to follow their reasoning.
2 Those who act quickly without thinking at all.

An incontinent person is like a city with good laws but no enforcement. A wicked person, by contrast, is like a city with bad laws that it actually follows. One is disorganized and weak, while the other is actively harmful.

- A self-controlled person sticks to their choices more than others do.
- An incontinent person follows their decisions less than most.

Impulsive incontinent people are easier to treat than those who think carefully yet don't act right.

Similarly, people who are incontinent due to habit are easier to fix than those who are naturally that way. Changing a habit is hard, but changing one's nature is even harder.

As the poet Evenus put it: *"Habit, long pursued, becomes our nature in the end."*

Pleasure

For philosophers, understanding pleasure and pain is key. It helps them decide what is good in life. Since happiness is often linked to pleasure, we must ask: Is pleasure truly good?

There are three main views:

1 All pleasure is bad. Some argue that pleasure is just a process, not a real goal.

2 Some pleasures are good, but most are bad. They claim that many pleasures are harmful or shameful.

3 Pleasure is good, but not the highest good. While

pleasure has value, life's ultimate goal must be something greater.

Those who argue against pleasure give several reasons:

• Pleasure is like building a house—it's just part of a
process, not an end goal.
• Smart people stay away from pleasure and focus on
self-control.
• Intelligent people aim to avoid pain rather than
chase pleasure.
• Extreme pleasures, like physical ones, can distract
us from thinking.
• No skill or art is devoted to creating pleasure, but
every good thing comes from skill.
• Even animals and children chase pleasure, which
makes it seem unworthy.

Is Pleasure Really Bad?

Even if some pleasures are harmful, that doesn't mean all
pleasure is bad.

• Context matters. Some things aren't always good,
but they can be good at the right time. For example,
medicine isn't enjoyable, but it's good when it heals
sickness.
• Not all pleasures fix a problem. Some, like learning
or thinking, exist simply because we are healthy and

whole. This shows pleasure isn't always a process—it can be part of a good life.

• A few bad examples don't define the whole. Some pleasures may be unhealthy, but that's like saying knowledge is bad just because some information is harmful.

• Wise people don't avoid all pleasure. They avoid excessive or harmful pleasures but still enjoy peace, learning, and deep thought.

Is Pleasure the Best Thing?

If pain is bad and should be avoided, then pleasure—its opposite—must be good. Some argue that pleasure and pain aren't true opposites, but this doesn't mean pleasure is bad.

Even if some pleasures are bad, pleasure itself can still be part of the highest good. People see knowledge as valuable, but some of it can be harmful. In the same way, the best pleasures—those tied to a good life—may be the highest good.

Happiness is supposed to be complete and perfect, and pleasure makes life better. Happy people still need good health, comfort, and good fortune. These things help remove obstacles that block the enjoyment of life. A person who is constantly suffering is not truly happy, even if they are a good person.

If pleasure weren't important, then a happy person wouldn't need it at all. But that would mean a happy person could be miserable, which doesn't make sense. So, a good life must also be a pleasurable one.

Are Most Pleasures Bad?

Some believe that only noble pleasures, such as learning and virtue, matter. They argue that bodily pleasures, like food, drink, and rest, are not worth choosing.

But if bodily pleasures aren't good, then why is bodily pain bad? If pain is bad, then its opposite—pleasure—should be good.

The key question is: Are necessary pleasures good, or just "not bad"?

- If something is good and can't be overdone, then its pleasure should also have no limit.
- If something can be excessive, then its pleasure can also be excessive.

Bodily pleasures can be taken too far, which is why some see them as bad. But a person isn't bad just because they enjoy necessary things. They become bad when they chase these pleasures in extreme ways.

Pain works differently. People don't just avoid too much pain—they try to avoid it entirely. But avoiding all pain isn't the same as avoiding all pleasure. Only people who chase extreme pleasure see pain as its direct opposite.

Why Do People Focus on Bodily Pleasures?

If bodily pleasures aren't the best ones, why do they seem more desirable?

1 They remove pain. People who are suffering seek strong pleasures to relieve their discomfort. The more painful their experience, the more extreme the pleasure they want.

2 Some come from bad habits or instincts. Some pleasures, like overeating or greed, may come from animal instincts or learned behavior.

3 They are intense. Some people cannot enjoy deeper, meaningful pleasures, so they focus on strong physical ones. They even create desires for themselves— like making themselves extra hungry just so they can enjoy food more.

4 People struggle with feeling neutral. When people aren't in pain or pleasure, they sometimes feel restless and crave excitement.

Scientists say that even simple actions, like seeing and hearing, can strain us a bit. But because we do these things all the time, we don't really notice. This may explain why people crave stronger pleasures—to break through the dullness of routine.

Young people, because they are growing, often feel restless—almost like they are "drunk with energy." This makes them naturally drawn to excitement and pleasure. People with high energy levels constantly seek stimulation, which can lead to bad habits.

Pain can be pushed away by a direct opposite pleasure, but also by any strong pleasure. Some people become self-indulgent. They seek pleasure to avoid discomfort.

The Two Types of Pleasure

There are two kinds of pleasure:

> 1 Pleasures that fix a problem – Like eating when
> you're starving or drinking when you're thirsty. These
> are only enjoyable because they remove discomfort.
> 2 Pleasures that stand alone are enjoying knowledge,
> friendship, and beauty. These are good in themselves,
> not just because they fix something.

Pleasures that come from pain have limits. If you're starving, there's a limit to how much food will satisfy you. But pleasures that don't come from pain—like learning or deep thinking—don't have limits.

Some pleasures are temporary, while others are lasting. If people had a simple and unchanging nature, they would always enjoy the same pleasure and wouldn't need variety. Some philosophers think God feels one perfect pleasure. Unlike humans, God doesn't need constant change to be happy.

People often say, "Change is sweet," because they crave variety. But constantly needing something new isn't always a good thing. A person who always seeks change may not be truly happy. People who crave excitement might feel restless. On the other hand, those who are genuinely good often find joy in stability.

Reflection & Application: Self-Control, Pleasure, and Living Well

Reflection Questions

- When do you struggle most with self-control? What helps you resist temptation?
- Have you ever done something you knew was wrong but couldn't stop yourself? Why?
- Do you think pleasure is necessary for happiness, or is it just a distraction?
- Can someone be too self-controlled? When might it be better to let go?
- How does anger affect your decisions compared to desire? Which is harder to control?
- Do you agree that chasing pleasure can sometimes be worse than getting angry? Why or why not?
- Do you seek pleasure because it truly makes you happy, or just because it removes discomfort?
- What's a pleasure that lasts for you—something that doesn't fade quickly? How can you focus more on that?

Actionable Steps

- ✓ Recognize your temptations. Notice when you give in to bad habits and reflect on why.
- ✓ Find better pleasures. Focus on lasting joys instead

of quick pleasures. Pick learning, relationships, or creativity instead of junk food and mindless scrolling.

✓ Practice mindful decision-making. Before acting on impulse, pause and ask: "Will this choice actually bring lasting happiness?"

✓ Don't confuse boredom with unhappiness. If you often look for distractions, try to enjoy stillness and stability.

✓ Train your willpower. Begin with small challenges, such as resisting a craving. This helps build self-discipline over time.

8

FRIENDSHIP

The Importance of Friendship

After discussing pleasure and pain, it makes sense to talk about friendship. Friendship is either a virtue or closely related to virtue, and it is one of the most important things in life.

No one would choose to live without friends, even if they had everything else—money, power, or success. In fact, the wealthiest and most powerful people seem to need friends the most. What is the point of having success if there is no one to share it with or no one to rely on? Friendship is essential for both enjoying life and protecting what we have. The more power or wealth a person has, the more risks they face, and the more they need friends they can trust.

Friendship is especially important during hard times.

• The poor or struggling see friends as their only
source of support.
• Young people rely on friends to help them stay out
of trouble.
• Older people need friends when they can no longer
do everything on their own.
• Those in their prime are encouraged by friendship
to do great things.

Even beyond its practical benefits, friendship is natural.
Parents love their children, and children love their parents—
not just in humans, but in animals as well. Even strangers
can feel connected simply because they share the bond of
being human. This is why travelers often find kindness in
unexpected places.

Friendship also holds entire communities together.
Lawmakers often value friendship over justice. When people
are friends, they don't need strict rules to get along. Even in
the most just society, friendship is still necessary. In fact, the
highest form of justice often looks a lot like friendship.

But friendship is not just useful—it is also noble. People
admire those who are loyal to their friends, and having many
friends is seen as a sign of a good person. This is why we
believe that good people naturally attract good friendships.

Do Similarities or Differences Bring People Together?

Many debates exist about friendship. Many think that similarity unites people. This idea leads to sayings like "birds of a

feather flock together."" Some believe opposites attract. They say people in the same job often compete instead of getting along.

Some philosophers take an even deeper approach:

• Euripides compared the earth and sky, saying they "love" each other because they provide what the other lacks.
• Heraclitus thought harmony arises from contrast. He said, "everything is born from struggle.""
• Empedocles, on the other hand, thought that similarity was what truly unites people.

We shouldn't focus on looks or outside traits. We should focus on what truly matters in friendship: character and feelings. The key questions are:

1 Can any two people be friends, or is true friendship only possible between good people?
2 Is there just one type of friendship, or are there different kinds?

Three Reasons for Love and What They Mean for Friendship

People don't love just anything—they love things that are:

• Good (things that make life better)
• Pleasant (things that bring joy)

• Useful (things that help them in some way)

Something useful is only valuable because it leads to something good or pleasant. So, in the end, people truly love either goodness or pleasure.

But love is not the same as friendship.

People do not have "friendship" with objects, even if they love them. No one says they "wish their wine well"—they just want it to stay in good condition so they can enjoy it. Friendship requires mutual care. It's not just about what one person wants, but about wishing good things for each other. If one person wishes another well in secret, they are not really friends if the other doesn't know.

The Three Types of Friendship

Friendship arises from goodness, pleasure, or usefulness. So, it shares the same roots as love.

1 Friendships of Usefulness

○ These friendships exist because both people benefit from each other.
○ The relationship is not based on who they are, but on what they can offer.
○ Often seen among business partners, co-workers, or political allies.
○ They are not deeply personal and tend to fade when the benefit disappears.

2 Friendships of Pleasure

○ These friendships form because people enjoy each other's company.

○ They are based on fun, entertainment, or shared interests.

○ Common among young people, who focus more on excitement than long-term bonds.

○ They can change quickly, as people's tastes and interests evolve.

3 Friendships of Virtue (True Friendship)

○ These friendships are based on mutual admiration and goodness.

○ The friends love each other for who they are, not for what they provide.

○ They are long-lasting because they are built on character, which does not change easily.

○ These friendships bring joy and help, but they run deeper. They are built on real respect and shared values.

True friendship is the most valuable because it lasts as long as both people remain good. However, it is also the rarest, because truly good people are hard to find.

The saying goes, "People cannot truly know each other until they have eaten salt together." This means real friendship needs time and shared experiences to grow. Those who quickly call someone their "best friend" may desire friendship, but they have not yet built a real one.

Let's look at the strengths and weaknesses of the different types of friendships we've explored.

Comparing True Friendship to Lesser Friendships

Perfect friendship is the strongest and most lasting because:

- It is based on equality—both friends give and receive equally.
- It is tested over time and built on trust.
- It does not fade when circumstances change.

Friendships that focus on pleasure or usefulness may seem like real friendships.

- A friendship between two funny people may seem deep, but it is really based on shared humor.
- A romantic relationship can struggle if one person craves attention while the other is eager to give it. If their roles shift, the bond may weaken.
- Business partners who work well together may seem close, but their bond may fade when the partnership ends.

Even bad people can form friendships based on pleasure or usefulness. They might entertain each other or help each other reach selfish goals. True friendship lasts and brings joy.

It only exists between good people who really care for one another.

One way to see the strength of true friendship is how it resists gossip. When two good people trust each other, they do not easily believe false rumors. Their loyalty is strong because they have proven their bond over time.

People call many types of relationships "friendships." So, it's important to understand their differences. The best friendship is between good people who love each other for who they are. Some friendships have qualities like true friendship. However, they aren't as deep or lasting.

Friendship as a State vs. Friendship as an Action

Some people are seen as good due to their character, while others are judged by their actions. Similarly, friendship can be viewed in two ways.

- Some people show friendship by spending time together. They help each other and enjoy each other's company.
- But even when friends are apart or asleep, they still have the potential to do these things.

Being apart doesn't end a friendship. However, it stops friends from showing it actively. However, if the separation lasts too long, they may begin to forget their bond. This is why people say, "Many friendships fade due to lack of conversation."

Older people and those with tough personalities find it hard to make friends. Friendship is based on enjoyment, and people naturally avoid what is unpleasant. No one wants to spend time with someone who is unfriendly. People who admire each other but don't spend time together aren't true friends. They are just nice to one another.

Spending time together is the strongest sign of friendship. Even those who have everything in life—wealth, power, and success—prefer not to be alone. True friendship often blooms among good people. Goodness and joy make someone lovable. Good people discover both in each other.

Friendship vs. Friendly Feelings

Loving someone is a feeling, while friendship is more of a character trait.

People can love lifeless things, like a favorite book or a stunning view. But true friendship needs choice. And choice comes from character.

Friendship is not just about feelings. It involves wishing good things for someone else for their own sake, not just for personal benefit. Good friends want the best for each other. They make each other's lives better. So, true friendship helps both people equally.

This is why friendship is often described as a kind of equality—and this is most true in the friendship of good people.

How Different Friendships Form

Enjoying each other's company is key to friendship. So, unfriendly or bitter people often struggle to make friends. Young people form friendships quickly because they are cheerful and open to fun. Older people often struggle more. They tend to care less about excitement and companionship.

However, even people who are not close friends may still have goodwill toward one another. They can wish each other well and help in tough times. But without shared experiences and fun, they aren't true friends.

How Many True Friends Can Someone Have?

You can't have a deep, perfect friendship with many people. It's like being deeply in love; you can't truly love many at once.

Love and deep friendship need strong feelings. These feelings usually center on one person, not many. It is difficult to admire and deeply connect with many people at the same time. True friendship takes time and familiarity to develop, and this is not easy to achieve with many people.

But, friendships based on utility or pleasure can involve many people. Many people can be useful or enjoyable to us, and such relationships require less time and commitment.

Friendships built on pleasure can feel more genuine. This is especially true when both friends share similar interests. Friendships that focus on usefulness often form between those who value business and practicality.

Even very happy and fulfilled people don't need friend-ships based on usefulness. They already have everything they need. But, they do seek out friendships based on plea-sure because even the happiest person does not want to live in isolation.

This is why happy people look for friends who are enjoy-able to be around. Ideally, their friends should also be good people, so they bring both pleasure and benefit to the rela-tionship.

Friendship Among the Powerful

People in positions of power often have different types of friends. Some are useful for handling responsibilities. Others are entertaining and enjoyable to be around.

It is rare for the same person to be both useful and pleasant in the way that true friendship requires. People in power usually pick fun, witty friends for enjoyment and practical ones for help. However, these traits rarely exist in one person.

A good person is friendly and helpful. However, they may struggle to form a close friendship with someone of higher status. This is only possible if that person also has great virtue. Without this balance, there is no equality in the rela-tionship.

Since it is rare to find people who surpass both in status and virtue, such friendships are uncommon.

Why Weaker Friendships Can Seem Like True Friendships

Friendships based on pleasure and utility involve a kind of balance. Friends give and receive the same things from each other—whether that's pleasure or a useful service. At times, one friend brings joy, while the other offers support.

However, these friendships are less stable than friendships based on virtue.

They are like true friendships. They bring joy and mutual benefit, just like virtuous friendships. But they lack deep trust and are easily broken when circumstances change. Unlike friendships of virtue, they do not stand the test of time.

Reciprocity of Friendship

Some friendships are unequal. For example, consider these types:

- Parents and children
- Older and younger people
- Rulers and subjects
- Husbands and wives

These friendships are not all the same.

The love between a father and son is different from that between a son and father. The love between a husband and wife isn't always equal. Each person plays a different role in the relationship.

Because of this, neither person should expect to give or receive exactly the same thing in return.

For example:

- Children should give their parents respect and gratitude.
- Parents should provide love, care, and guidance.

When both sides do their part, the friendship stays strong and lasts.

In unequal friendships, love should be proportional. The better or more important person should receive more love than they give. The more useful person should be appreciated more in return. This creates a sense of balance, which is necessary for friendship to work.

However, equality in friendship is not the same as equality in justice. In justice, fairness is based on merit—people get what they deserve based on their abilities or contributions. In friendship, equality is more about emotional balance.

Can Friendship Exist Between People Who Are Too Different?

If two people are too unequal, their friendship cannot last.

For example, humans cannot be friends with the gods

because the gods are far above them in every way. Common people do not expect to be friends with kings. Most people don't think they can have close friendships with wise or extraordinary individuals.

It is difficult to say how much inequality a friendship can handle before it stops being a friendship.

A big difference can't always end a friendship right away. But if one person grows distant in status, intelligence, or character, the bond can fade.

Some people ask, "Should I wish my friends the best success, even if they outshine me and leave me behind?""

The answer is that a true friend wishes for their friend's success, but not in a way that makes friendship impossible. A person does not wish for their friend to become something so different that the friendship disappears.

Loving Is More Essential to Friendship Than Being Loved

Most people prefer to be loved rather than to love because being loved makes them feel honored. People like flattery because flatterers pretend to care more than they do. This makes others feel valued.

But, people don't seek honor for its own sake. Instead, they want what honor represents. Some want recognition from those in power because they believe it will lead to future rewards. Others seek honor from wise and virtuous people because it reassures them that they are truly good.

But being loved is different. People enjoy being loved for

its own sake, not because of any future benefit. This suggests that love itself is better than honor and that friendship is valuable on its own.

The Virtue of Loving in Friendship

Friendship is not just about being loved—it is about loving.

This is clear in the way mothers love their children. Some mothers give up their children to be raised by others, yet they still love them, even if the children do not love them back. These mothers do not seek love in return; they simply find joy in knowing their children are happy.

This shows that loving is more important than being loved in friendship. The best and most lasting friendships are those where both people love each other equally and sincerely.

People who love their friends are the ones truly praised, proving that loving is the real virtue of friendship.

This explains why unequal friendships can exist. The love between friends adjusts to match their roles. The strongest friendships form between those who are similar in virtue. Good people stay true to themselves. They help each other grow. Wicked people, on the other hand, often change their desires and friendships. They lack stability.

Why Friendships Between Bad People Don't Last

Friendships between bad people fall apart quickly. They do not stay true to their own values, so they cannot be loyal to others. They become friends by enjoying each other's bad behavior. But when their desires change, their friendship fades away.

Friendships built on pleasure or usefulness tend to last longer than those among bad people. However, they only last as long as the benefits keep coming.

Friendships of utility often form between opposites. For example, they can exist between the rich and the poor or between those who know a lot and those who know little.

In these relationships, each person gives what the other needs. They trade what they have to offer.

The same goes for romantic relationships. One person might be beautiful while the other isn't. Also, one could be older and the other younger.

Some romantic relationships can seem silly. One person, who may not have much to love, asks for equal affection. This can feel unfair to the other partner. If both people are equally lovable, their love is justified—but if they are not, the relationship seems foolish.

Opposites may not attract as much as it seems—rather, people seek those who help them achieve balance in life. For example, a dry object does not naturally seek to become soaking wet but rather aims for an ideal level of moisture. Friendships often grow between people who complement each other, not just opposites. Friendships may work the same way. People often seek those who help them lead a balanced and good life, rather than their opposites. However, this idea belongs to another discussion and is not the main concern of friendship.

Friendship and Fairness in Communities

Friendship and fairness (justice) go together. They apply to the same people and work in similar ways.

In every kind of community, people expect fairness, and they also form friendships.

Travelers and soldiers often call each other "friends." They do this because they share experiences and depend on each other.

The stronger the connection, the deeper the friendship and the greater the sense of fairness.

There is a saying: "Friends share everything." This is because friendship is based on having things in common. Close friends, like brothers, share almost everything. Some relationships involve less sharing. It depends on their nature.

Because friendships come in different forms, so do expectations of fairness.

- Parents treat their children in a unique way, unlike how brothers treat one another.
- Fellow citizens have different obligations than strangers.
- Betraying a friend is worse than deceiving a stranger.
- Harming a family member is worse than hurting someone you barely know.

The closer the friendship, the greater the expectation of loyalty and fairness.

The Role of Friendship in Society

All smaller communities are part of a larger political community (the state). People join groups to achieve common goals. This can be for survival, success, or shared interests. The state exists to help all its citizens. Lawmakers aim to create fair rules for everyone.

Sailors, soldiers, and local communities come together for key reasons:

- Sailors work as a team to make a living.
- Soldiers fight for victory.
- Citizens help each other stay safe.

Some groups exist for fun. These include social clubs and religious gatherings. These also fit into the state's bigger picture. It's not just about short-term gains. It's about improving life overall.

Types of Government and How They Change

There are three main types of good government, each with a corrupt version that develops when the system goes wrong.

The Three Good Governments

1 Monarchy – Rule by one wise and virtuous leader.
2 Aristocracy – Rule by a small group of capable and fair-minded people.

3 Timocracy (or Polity) – Rule by qualified citizens, often based on property or standards.

Among these, monarchy is considered the best, while timocracy is the least ideal.

The Three Corrupt Governments

Each good system has a flawed version:

- Tyranny is monarchy gone wrong. A tyrant rules for himself, while a true king rules for the people. Because a real king already has everything he needs, he focuses on others. A tyrant, however, just wants more power, making tyranny the worst form of government.
- Oligarchy is aristocracy gone wrong. Instead of wise rulers acting for the common good, an oligarchy is controlled by a few selfish people who favor the rich.
- Democracy is timocracy gone wrong. It's not as harmful as tyranny or oligarchy, but it has flaws. It gives power to the majority, but they don't always choose the best leaders. Democracy is a bit like timocracy. Because of this, it is the least harmful among corrupt systems.

How Governments Change Over Time

Governments change with new leaders and shifts in society.

- Monarchies turn into tyrannies when kings become selfish.
- Oligarchies arise from aristocracies. This happens when leaders focus on wealth and power.
- Timocracies turn into democracies when more people want equal rights.

Political changes are like family relationships.

- Monarchy is like a father leading a family—when just, he cares for his children; when unjust, he becomes a tyrant.
- Aristocracy resembles a balanced marriage. The husband leads in certain areas but also respects his wife's strengths. If he controls everything unfairly, it becomes an oligarchy.
- Timocracy is like brothers—mostly equal but with small differences. If one brother is much older or stronger, equality fades.
- Democracy exists in a home where parents have less control, and everyone acts on their own.

Friendship in Different Governments

Different governments have their own ideas of fairness. They also have various types of friendship.

- In a monarchy, the friendship between the ruler and the people is based on generosity. A good king looks after his people, much like a father cares for his children. Parents are honored because they provide life and guidance.
- In an aristocracy, friendship is like a good marriage —the more capable person leads, but both benefit fairly.
- In a timocracy, friendship feels like brotherhood. Citizens share rights and take turns leading.

Friendship in Corrupt Governments

- Tyranny has the weakest friendship. Just as there is no friendship between a master and his tools, a tyrant treats people as objects.
- Oligarchy has some friendship, but only between the wealthy few, not the common people.
- Democracy builds strong friendships. In a democracy, all citizens are equal. This equality boosts justice and loyalty in society.

Family and Friendship

Every type of friendship is based on some kind of connection. Family friendships are stronger than other bonds. They are deeper than those with neighbors or travel partners.

Why Parents Love Their Children More Than Children Love Their Parents

Parents love their children because they see them as part of themselves. Children, on the other hand, love their parents because they come from them. But this love is not equal:

- Parents know their kids from the start. But kids need time to grasp their bond with parents.
- Parents feel ownership over their children, much like a person sees their own hair or teeth as part of them. But a child does not "own" their parent in the same way.
- Love develops over time. Parents love their kids from birth. But children learn to love as they grow and understand more.

Mothers often love their children more deeply than fathers. This is because they share a closer physical connection at birth.

Friendship Between Siblings and Relatives

Brothers love each other because they come from the same parents. People describe family members as being "of the same blood" or "the same stock" because they share a natural bond.

Growing up together and being close in age strengthens friendship. Siblings who share experiences develop lifelong connections.

Cousins and other relatives share family ties. However, their closeness varies based on how they are related.

Friendship Based on Respect and Gratitude

Children's friendships with their parents are like how people connect with the gods. Both are built on respect and gratitude. Parents provide life, care, and education—the greatest gifts a person can receive. These friendships are often nicer and more helpful than those with strangers. Family members live together and share more experiences.

The friendship between brothers is also like that of close friends, especially when they are good people. Brothers:

- Start with a natural love for each other from birth.
- Often grow up together with shared experiences.
- Have their friendship tested and proven over time.

Family relationships can show friendship in various ways. This depends on how closely related the people are.

The Friendship Between Husband and Wife

Friendship between a man and a woman is natural. People are drawn to form couples even before they build cities or create governments. Families come first, and all living creatures share the instinct to reproduce. Human relationships are different from those of animals. They extend beyond just reproduction.

Men and women live together for many reasons. Right from the start, they take on different roles. These roles help them work together and improve their lives. Marriage brings both benefits, like supporting one another, and joy, like having fun together.

A marriage based on virtue, however, is the strongest. When both partners are good people, they support and bring out the best in each other. They don't just benefit from the relationship; they genuinely enjoy each other's goodness.

Children also strengthen the bond between husband and wife. Childless couples often separate more easily. Without kids, there's no bond keeping them together. Children belong to both parents and create a lasting link between them.

Friendship and Fairness in Relationships

How people treat their friends, family members, and spouses is closely connected to fairness. Different relationships need different types of fairness. What you owe a close friend isn't the same as what you owe a stranger. A classmate is treated differently than a lifelong companion.

Friendship has many forms, so it also has different rules of fairness. This is especially important in friendships where people are equals or have differences.

Moral Dilemmas in Friendship

As discussed before, there are three kinds of friendship:

- Friendship based on virtue (deep and lasting, between good people)
- Friendship based on pleasure (enjoying each other's company)
- Friendship based on usefulness (benefiting from each other's help)

In a fair friendship, both friends give and receive equally. This applies to love, support, and effort. If one gives more and receives little in return, the friendship can become unbalanced.

Friends can argue when they both want something from each other. Friendships based on virtue rely on goodwill. In contrast, useful friendships can lead to competition. Each person may try to get more than they give, leading to frustration.

Friendships based on usefulness can be compared to justice, which has two forms:

- Legal justice – Clear rules and agreements, like contracts or business deals.

• Moral justice means following unwritten social
rules, such as returning a favor.

Friendships of usefulness also fall into these two
categories:

• Legal friendships – Based on clear agreements.
Some involve direct exchanges, like paying for a
service. Others are favors that people expect to repay
later.
• Moral friendships – Based on goodwill, but often
with an expectation of future help. If one person feels
they gave more than they received, they may feel
cheated.

People like to appear generous, but they often choose
what benefits them the most. While it is noble to give
without expecting anything in return, it is more convenient
to receive without repaying. This is why people often
accept favors while secretly hoping they won't have to
return them.

To avoid conflict, it's best to repay what you receive when-
ever possible. If you took a favor thinking there were no
strings attached, it's best to own up to that mistake. Then,
return the kindness. If repayment is impossible, then even
the giver wouldn't expect it to be done.

Another debate is how to measure the value of a favor:

The recipient may say, "It was easy for you to help me—
you would have done it for anyone."

The giver may say, "It was a big sacrifice, and no one else would have helped you."

In friendships of usefulness, repayment should be based on the recipient's benefit. If the favor was given expecting something in return, the recipient should give back the same or even more. That would be even kinder. However, in friendships based on virtue, repayment isn't necessary. True friendship is about goodwill, not transactions.

Friendship Between Unequals

Friendships with one person being better in wisdom, wealth, or power can cause disagreements. Both sides may feel they deserve more from the relationship:

- The superior friend may expect more respect for their contributions.
- The inferior friend may expect more help since the other has more resources.

To maintain balance, each person should receive what fits their role:

- The superior friend should receive honor and respect.
- The inferior friend should receive help or material support.

This balance also applies to society. Leaders and helpers

get recognition, but those in need get support. Officials get recognition, but workers earn their pay in money. No one wants to receive less in every way, so friendship stays strong when there is a fair exchange of honor and material benefits.

This idea also applies to friendships. People who get help —be it money, support, or advice—should express thanks and respect in return. Even if they can't fully repay the favor, they should make an effort.

For example, children can never fully repay their parents for giving them life and raising them. However, they should still honor and support their parents as much as they can. Friendship does not ask for perfect equality—only that each person does what is possible.

A son might find it hard to repay his father's sacrifices. In some cases, a father may decide to distance himself from a troubled son. A child remains deeply connected to their parents, as their upbringing shapes their entire life.

In most cases, though, parents do not reject their children unless the child has done something truly terrible. A father has a natural bond with his child, and human nature makes it hard to reject a son, even if he is disappointing.

However, a wicked son may neglect or abandon his father. Most people want to receive benefits, but they avoid giving them when they see no personal gain. Selfishness makes people leave relationships when they no longer serve their needs.

Reflection & Application: Friendship

Reflection Questions

• Do you think most of your friendships are based on utility, pleasure, or virtue?

• Have you ever had a friendship that faded when the benefit disappeared? What did you learn from that experience?

• How do you maintain long-term friendships? What do you think is the key to lasting connection?

• Have you ever had a friendship that felt unequal? How did you handle it?

• Do you agree that loving is more important than being loved in friendship? Why or why not?

• How does friendship play a role in justice in your community, workplace, or personal life?

• What steps can you take to be a better friend and build deeper, more meaningful friendships?

Actionable Steps

✓ Invest in friendships of virtue. Find people who inspire you to be better and value character over entertainment or benefits.

✓ Strengthen your friendships through shared experiences. Spend time together, talk deeply, and support each other's growth.

✓ Recognize when friendships are fading. If a friendship is based on utility or pleasure, accept that it might not last forever.

✓ Be the kind of friend you want to have. Offer loyalty, honesty, and care without expecting something in return.

✓ Balance unequal friendships with respect. In relationships with power differences, it's better to show appreciation and respect. Instead of demanding equal treatment, focus on honoring the other person.

✓ Understand that friendships evolve. Just because a friendship changes doesn't mean it wasn't meaningful. Let go gracefully when necessary.

9

FRIENDSHIP (CONTINUED)

Principles to Be Observed When Friends Have Different Motives

Friendships can be hard when friends expect different things. When one person enjoys a relationship for fun, and the other sees it as a way to gain something, misunderstandings happen. This imbalance often leads to complaints:

• A lover may feel they are giving too much affection without receiving the same love in return.

• A beloved may feel the person who once promised them everything is no longer fulfilling their promises.

Conflicts arise when people don't love each other for who they are. Instead, they focus on qualities like beauty, pleasure, or usefulness. These things don't last forever. When these qualities fade or don't provide the expected benefits, the friendship weakens. Friendships built on character last longer. They don't rely on temporary qualities.

A similar issue occurs when what is given is not what was expected. There's an old story about a man who promised great rewards to a musician if he played beautifully. The musician played well. He expected to be paid. But the next morning, the man refused. He said the musician had already been "paid" with the joy of performing. Misunderstandings occur when people expect different things from each other in a relationship. For example, if one person seeks fun but the other wants a reward, their views will clash.

Who Decides the Value of a Service?

Should the giver decide what their service was worth, or should the receiver?

In some cases, the receiver sets the price. For instance, the philosopher Protagoras taught students. He let them choose the value of his lessons. Some believe it is better to set a fixed price in advance to avoid disagreements later.

People who promise a service but fail to deliver what was expected naturally cause complaints. This is why some criticize those who take payment first but do not fulfill their promises. Some say sophists, who teach rhetoric and philosophy, fit this idea. They charge high fees, but their students often feel they learned nothing useful.

If there's no formal agreement, people who give something freely shouldn't be blamed. This is especially true in friendships based on virtue. In these friendships, help comes from goodwill, not from expecting something in return. In these cases, repayment should reflect the giver's original intentions. In true friendship, the reason behind the act is more important than the act itself.

This is true for relationships with teachers too, especially those who teach philosophy. Their value cannot be measured in money, and they often do not receive the level of honor they deserve. Just as we cannot fully repay our parents or the gods, we should still give teachers what we can as a sign of gratitude.

If a gift comes with an expectation of repayment, both sides should agree on a fair way to settle the debt. However, if no agreement can be reached, then the person who received the benefit should decide what the return should be. In business, buyers often set the value of goods based on what they are willing to pay. Similarly, fairness in friendship should be based on the original need and the benefit received.

Disputes about value often come up in transactions, but friendships lead to even tougher questions. When different obligations conflict, how do we decide who deserves our help first?

Who Should We Help First?

Sometimes, we must choose who to help first when we have multiple obligations. These decisions can be tough.

- Should you obey your father or follow a doctor's advice when sick?

- Should you give a job to a friend or to the most qualified person?
- Should you repay someone who helped you before or help a friend in need?

Moral duties are like debts—we should repay past help before taking on new obligations. However, exceptions exist. If a man is saved from kidnappers, should he save his rescuer or his father first? In some cases, helping family takes priority.

If someone once loaned money to a dishonest person, should they lend to them again? Fairness is about character. It doesn't rely on past help or favors, even from dishonest people.

How to Divide Duties Among Different Relationships

Not all duties should go to the same person. Just as gods need special offerings, relationships need different types of support:

- Parents need care and support because they give life and nurture us.
- Parents and the gods should receive honor, but in different ways—one does not honor a father the same way as a general or a philosopher.
- Older people deserve respect, such as standing when they enter a room or offering them a seat.
- Siblings and close friends need to feel familiar with

each other. They crave openness and shared moments together.
• Treat relatives, friends, and acquaintances according to your closeness, their character, and how useful they are.

Some choices are easier, such as prioritizing one family member over another. Others, like choosing between a friend and a benefactor, are harder. Still, fairness requires that we make these decisions carefully and justly.

When Should a Friendship End?

Should a friendship end if a person changes?

• Friendships based on fun or usefulness often fade when those things disappear.
• It's unfair to pretend to love someone for who they are when we only care about what they offer.
• Conflicts happen when people think a friendship is deeper than it actually is.

If a person turns bad, should their friend still love them? No one should be expected to love something evil. If the bad friend can change, a true friend should try to help. But if they are completely wicked, the friendship should end.

As people grow, their values change. A childhood friendship may fade if one friend matures and wants deeper goals, while the other still focuses on simple pleasures. This is common as people outgrow each other.

Even if a friendship ends, an old friend should not be treated like a stranger. Past friendships deserve respect, unless they ended due to serious wrongdoing.

Internal Nature of Friendship

The way we treat our friends is a lot like the way we treat ourselves. A good friend cares about someone else, wants the best for them, and shares in their happiness and struggles. This kind of friendship is easy to see in how a mother loves her child.

A good person feels this way about themselves, too. They like who they are and make choices that match their values. They love being alone. They think about their past with pride and look to the future with excitement. Since a friend is "another self," true friendship is a reflection of self-love.

But not everyone feels this way. Some people struggle with themselves. A person who is often selfish or does bad things may feel regret, guilt, or inner conflict. For example:

- Someone who knows junk food is bad for them but eats too much of it anyway feels torn between what they want and what they know is right.
- A person who lies to their friends may feel bad later, but their desire for attention or approval keeps them doing it.

People who feel this way don't enjoy being alone. They distract themselves with others to avoid thinking about their actions. Because they don't truly love themselves, they can't have deep, lasting friendships. This is why real friendship only happens between good people—those who live in a way they can be proud of.

Friendship reflects self-love. So, it makes sense that goodwill, the first step to friendship, shows how we treat ourselves.

How Friendship and Goodwill Are Connected

Goodwill is like the first step toward friendship, but it's not the same thing. You can feel goodwill for someone you don't know well. For example, you might wish a classmate luck on a test. But this doesn't mean you're close friends.

Goodwill is different from deep friendship because:

• It doesn't require spending time together or sharing experiences.
• It can appear suddenly, like when people cheer for an underdog in a sports game.
• It's more like wishing someone well rather than truly caring about them.

Goodwill can become real friendship. This happens when it lasts and shows true care for the other person. It's not just about being useful or fun to be around.

Friendship and Harmony

Friends usually get along because they share similar ideas and goals. This is called concord, which means agreement and harmony. But just agreeing on random things—like the weather or favorite foods—isn't true concord. Real harmony happens when people work toward the same goal and want the best for each other.

For example:

- A school group working on a project together agrees on who should do what, making their team-work smooth.
- Citizens in a country agree on fair laws that help everyone, leading to a peaceful society.

Good people create the strongest harmony because they are fair and want justice for everyone. But selfish people struggle with this. They want the best for themselves. But they also avoid responsibility. This causes fights and unfairness.

Why People Love Helping Others

Have you ever noticed that people who help others often feel happier than those who just receive help? Helpers, like parents, teachers, or friends who share lunch, often care more for others than those people do for them.

This might seem strange, but it happens for a few reasons:

- When people do something kind, they see a part of themselves in that act—just like a baker feels proud of a cake they made.
- Giving help makes people feel like they've created something good in the world, and that feels rewarding.
- It's more satisfying to remember something good you've done than just to receive a favor.

This is why parents often love their children more than children love their parents. A mother puts in so much effort —carrying, feeding, and caring for a baby—that she naturally feels a strong bond. Fathers love their children, too. However, they don't experience the same physical effort as mothers. So, their connection might feel different.

People also love things they worked hard for more than things they got easily. For example, a person who saved up for a bike may treasure it more than someone who was simply given one. In the same way, those who help others feel more connected to the people they helped than the other way around.

The Nature of True Self-Love

Some people think self-love is selfish. Greedy people care only about their success, power, or pleasure. But good people put their friends, family, and community before themselves.

So, is self-love bad? It depends on what kind of self-love we mean:

- Selfish self-love: When people only care about money, power, or pleasure.
- Good self-love: When people choose wisdom, kindness, and fairness over selfish desires.

A good person may give up wealth or even risk their life for what is right—not because they think less of themselves, but because noble actions are the best choices.

So, should people love themselves? Yes—but in the way a good person does, not in a selfish way.

The Need for Friendship

Why does the happy man need friends?

Some people wonder whether a truly happy person even needs friends. If someone is already completely happy and has everything they need, why would they need anyone else? After all, isn't a friend just someone who fills in what a person lacks?

But this idea doesn't quite make sense. If happiness is about having everything good, wouldn't that include friendship? And if friendship is about doing good for others, wouldn't a happy person want the chance to do that?

So, do we need friends more in good times or bad times?

Some say friends are most useful when life is hard. Others believe friends are needed in good times, too, because happiness is best when shared.

A truly happy person would not want to be alone. Even if they don't need friends for survival, they would still want to experience life with others.

Some people believe happy people don't need friends. They might only see friendships as useful or enjoyable. It's true that a self-sufficient person doesn't need friends to help them or entertain them. But that doesn't mean they don't need true friendship, which is based on character and goodness.

Since happiness is something we practice in daily life, a happy person wants to share it. Watching a friend do good things is one of life's greatest pleasures. A happy person enjoys seeing virtue in others, just as they enjoy living a good life themselves. Life is more enjoyable with friends. A person alone may struggle to always stay active, but with friends, they can share experiences, thoughts, and fun. Being around good people encourages virtue. A wise person enjoys having wise friends, just as a strong person enjoys training with strong teammates.

Humans are naturally social. Even animals like to be in groups, so how much more do people need companionship? A good life is not just about living—it's about being aware of how good life is. That awareness is strongest when we share it with others.

How Many Friends Should We Have?

Is it better to have as many friends as possible, or just a few? There's an old saying that warns against having too many or too few.

For useful friendships, this makes sense. Too many can be overwhelming because keeping up with all those connections takes time and effort. If a person is constantly helping others or repaying favors, they won't have time to focus on what really matters. The same goes for friendships based on pleasure—a few good ones are enough, like adding just the right amount of seasoning to food.

But what about true, noble friendships? Should we have as many as possible, or is there a limit?

A city can't be too small or too large—less than ten people wouldn't make a real city, but too many would be impossible to manage. Friendship is the same. The right number of friends is the number you can actually spend time with and share life with.

Real friendship takes time. If a person has too many close friends, they won't be able to give each one the attention they deserve. True friendship requires deep affection. If someone tries to be close to everyone, they may end up being close to no one. Large friend groups rarely make deep connections. Most famous friendships in history involve only two people, not big groups.

We can have many casual friends, like classmates, teammates, or neighbors. But true, deep friendship is rare. If a person finds even a few great friends in life, they should consider themselves lucky.

Do We Need Friends More in Good Times or Bad?

People turn to friendship in both good and bad times, but for different reasons.

In hard times, friends are needed for support. They help us through struggles, share our burdens, and bring comfort when we are suffering. Even if they can't solve our problems, just having them near makes things easier.

In good times, friends make life more enjoyable. Success feels greater when shared, and their happiness for us adds to our own. True friendship is not just about receiving help but about sharing kindness and generosity.

This means that friendship is more essential in hardship but more noble in success.

The Comfort of Friends in Hard Times

Seeing a friend when we are struggling is reassuring. Their presence can protect us from despair because they understand us and know how to lift our spirits. However, there is also a challenge—our suffering can cause them pain.

Some people avoid sharing their troubles because they don't want their friends to suffer alongside them. Many find comfort in grieving together, especially those who feel deeply. Neither approach is wrong, but it is wise to follow the example of those who handle hardship with strength and grace.

A good rule is to only ask for help when it is truly needed. There's an old saying: *"My misfortune is enough for me."* This reminds us not to burden others unless their help will make a real difference.

At the same time, a true friend doesn't wait to be asked. It is more noble to offer help freely, especially when someone is in great need. This kindness benefits both the giver and the receiver.

Friendship in Times of Success

In times of prosperity, friendship takes on a different role. Friends make happiness even greater just by being part of it. Generosity is noble, so we should gladly invite friends to share in our good fortune. However, we should not be too quick to take favors from our successful friends—it's unworthy to only receive but never give.

At the same time, we shouldn't refuse their kindness too harshly. Rejecting a friend's generosity can create distance and make them feel unappreciated. A balance must be found —accepting kindness with gratitude while always being ready to give in return.

Friends help each other in tough times and good times. They also want to share life experiences together. The highest joy of friendship is not just support, but shared existence.

The Best Part of Friendship: Living Together

Lovers find their greatest joy in simply seeing the one they love. In the same way, friends find happiness in each other's presence. Friendship is a kind of partnership, and just as we naturally want to be aware of our own lives, we also want to be aware of our friends' lives. This is why friends seek to spend time together—it is how they truly share life.

Whatever people value most, they want to do with their friends. Some drink or gamble together. Others exercise, hunt, or study philosophy. The activities they love most are the ones they want to share.

This is why bad friendships can be dangerous—bad people encourage bad behavior. If friends do harmful things together, they make each other worse. But friendships between good people are different. They improve each other, shaping their character like a craftsman shapes his work. That's why people say, *"Noble deeds come from noble men."*

Friendship is not just a part of a good life—it is essential to it. Happiness comes from living well. Living well is best when shared, so friendship makes the human experience whole. Now, let us turn to pleasure, another powerful force in shaping the good life.

Reflection & Application: Balancing Friendships

Reflection Questions

• Have you ever had a friendship where both of you expected different things? How did it turn out?

• Have you ever outgrown a friendship? Did it end naturally or was there conflict?

• How do you decide who to prioritize when helping friends, family, or mentors?

• Do you agree that self-love is essential for true friendship? Why or why not?

• Have you ever struggled to accept help from a friend? How did it make you feel?

• Do you think friendship is more important in good times or bad times?

Actionable Steps

✓ Communicate expectations clearly. If one friend is serious while the other just wants fun, be honest about your needs.

✓ Choose quality over quantity. Deep friendships take time—don't spread yourself too thin.

✓ Practice good self-love. Take care of yourself so you can bring your best self to your friendships.

✓ Accept change. If a friendship fades due to life changes, let it go with respect instead of forcing it.

✓ Balance giving and receiving. Be generous, but don't let yourself be taken advantage of. Accept kindness with gratitude.

✓ Spend time with good people. Surround yourself

with friends who help you grow, not those who bring
you down.

✔ Enjoy friendship for its own sake. Friendship isn't
just about helping or being helped—it's about
sharing life.

10

PLEASURE, HAPPINESS

Pleasure

Few things shape human life as much as pleasure. It guides our choices, influences our character, and affects our happiness. But this power also makes it controversial. Is pleasure the highest good, or can it lead us astray? For centuries, philosophers have debated this topic. They offer various views on its importance in living a good life.

Pleasure plays a major role in human life. It influences our choices, shapes our virtues, and affects our happiness. This is why we teach children using pleasure and pain—guiding them to enjoy what is good and avoid what is harmful.

Because pleasure is so powerful, people have debated its value for centuries.

- Some believe pleasure is the highest good, arguing that since all living things seek it, it must be the ultimate goal.
- Some say pleasure is completely bad. They think that avoiding pleasure helps people control their desires.
- Some reject pleasure not because they believe it is bad, but because they fear that praising it will lead people to excess.

However, denying the reality of pleasure is not a good approach. People might ignore arguments that go against clear facts. If someone speaks out against pleasure but is later seen enjoying it, others may think all pleasure is good.

A better approach is to explore the truth about pleasure —what kind is good, what kind is bad, and whether it is the highest good in life.

Is Pleasure the Highest Good?

Eudoxus, the philosopher, believed pleasure is the highest good. He argued that all living things naturally seek pleasure. Just as a plant reaches for sunlight and an animal hunts for food, people instinctively seek out pleasure. If nature guides all beings toward what is best for them, then pleasure must be the highest and most natural goal..

His argument was very convincing due to his character. Eudoxus was known for his self-control. Because of this, people thought he defended pleasure not for personal desire but for reason.

He supported his argument with several points:

- Pleasure is universal—all creatures seek it and avoid pain.
- Pleasure is chosen for its own sake, not as a means to something else (just like happiness).
- Pleasure improves good things. It makes justice and wisdom even more appealing.

Plato disagreed. He argued that if pleasure were truly the highest good, it would be self-sufficient—needing nothing to improve it. But we see that pleasure is made better by wisdom and virtue. If something requires another good to complete it, then it cannot be the highest good. Wisdom, not pleasure, is what makes life truly fulfilling.

One more point against pleasure as the ultimate good is its lack of a fixed limit. People feel pleasure in different amounts. But this argument is weak, since the same could be said of justice or courage. Just because something exists in degrees doesn't mean it isn't real or valuable.

In the end, pleasure is clearly good, but whether it is the *greatest* good remains uncertain.

Is Pleasure Entirely Bad?

Some philosophers argue that pleasure is not truly good because it is just a process—like hunger being satisfied by food. If pleasure is simply the filling of a need, then it is not valuable on its own.

But this argument doesn't match reality. Many pleasures do not come from relief of pain.

- The joy of learning something new.
- The delight of hearing beautiful music.
- The satisfaction of remembering happy moments.

These pleasures do not arise from suffering but are good in themselves.

Some people say pleasure is bad. They think some pleasures can cause shame. But just because some pleasures are bad does not mean all are. Wealth can be earned dishonorably, but wealth itself is not bad. Pleasure can come from dishonorable actions, but pleasure itself is not bad.

The key difference is where the pleasure comes from. The pleasure of a just person differs from that of a corrupt person. The joy of a musician differs from that of someone who has no appreciation for music.

Not all pleasure is equal. The source of the pleasure matters.

This is why people respect true friends but look down on flatterers. A friend supports us because they care, while a flatterer only seeks to please us. Pleasure alone is not enough —it must be tied to something good.

Another test:

- No one would choose to live with the mind of a child forever, even if it meant endless pleasure.
- No one would want to gain pleasure through disgraceful actions, even if there were no consequences.

This shows that there are things we value even beyond pleasure—like virtue, knowledge, and meaning. Pleasure is not the highest good, but it is not entirely bad either. Some pleasures are genuinely good, while others should be avoided.

Understanding the Nature of Pleasure

To fully understand pleasure, we must ask: What kind of experience is it?

Some claim that pleasure is a movement—like walking from one place to another. But this idea doesn't hold up.

How is pleasure different from movement?

- A movement has a starting point and an end goal.
- A pleasure is complete in each moment—it does not need an end to be fully experienced.

For example:

- Building a house is a movement. It takes time, and each step (laying bricks, adding the roof) is different from the finished house.

• Seeing a beautiful view is not a movement. At any moment, the experience is whole.

Pleasure is like seeing—it is already complete in itself. This is why it is not a process or a movement but a kind of experience that is fully present in every instant.

How Pleasure Relates to Activity

Every sense functions in relation to its proper object. The best experience occurs when our senses connect with the ideal object. A musician loves a perfectly tuned melody. A philosopher grasps a deep truth. Such activity is not only complete but also pleasurable.

Pleasure doesn't cause the activity, but it makes it better. It's like how youth's glow makes a healthy person look even more beautiful.

Why Doesn't Pleasure Last Forever?

• Pleasure comes from being active, but people can't stay active all the time.
• Just as our bodies tire, so do our minds.
• Some things excite us at first but lose their appeal over time because our initial engagement fades.

People desire pleasure because they desire life itself. Life is a kind of activity, and each person enjoys the activities they value most:

- A musician finds joy in music.
- A scholar enjoys learning.
- A thinker delights in understanding deep truths.

Since pleasure enhances activity, it also enhances life itself. This is why pleasure and happiness are so closely connected.

Different Kinds of Pleasure

Pleasures differ because the activities they go with are different. Just like tools are made for specific jobs, animals have unique roles in nature. So too, different activities need different kinds of pleasure.

How Pleasure Affects Learning and Growth

People who enjoy a subject learn it more quickly—pleasure sharpens focus and effort. But, external pleasures can weaken an activity. A music lover might struggle to focus on a serious conversation if music is playing in the background. A strong pleasure can overpower a weaker one.

Good vs. Bad Pleasures

Since some activities are noble and others are harmful, the pleasures connected to them also differ:

- Pleasure from virtuous actions is good.

• Pleasure from vice is bad.

A just person enjoys justice, just as a musical person enjoys music. But, someone with bad habits may crave pleasures that are not truly good—just as a sick person might crave unhealthy food.

Pleasure comes from activity. So, the best pleasures arise from our highest activities: wisdom and virtue.

Happiness

We've talked about virtue, friendship, and pleasure. Now, let's discuss happiness—the main goal of life.

Happiness is not just feeling good or doing nothing. If it were, someone who sleeps all the time or has a tough life could still be happy, which doesn't make sense. Instead, happiness is something we do—an activity.

There are two types of activities:

• Some are done for a reason, like working to earn money.
• Others are valuable on their own, like being kind just because it's right.

Happiness is part of the second group. It is complete, meaning we choose it for itself, not for something else.

Why Fun Isn't the Same as Happiness

Some people think happiness comes from amusement, like games and entertainment. But fun can be distracting—it can make people ignore their health and responsibilities.

- Many believe powerful people (like kings or tyrants) are happy because they have fun.
- But having power doesn't mean they make good choices.
- A good person sees value in things that truly matter, so real happiness must come from virtue.

Happiness Comes from Virtue

Life isn't about working hard just so we can play. That would be silly! Instead:

- Most things we do lead to something greater—except happiness, which is the final goal.
- Resting is important, but only so we can return to meaningful activities.
- Serious and meaningful things matter more than silly or fun things.

Even a slave can enjoy physical pleasures, but that's not true happiness unless they also live a full and good life.

The Contemplative Life is the Happiest

If happiness comes from living well, then the happiest life must come from the highest virtue.

The best part of us—our ability to think and understand—allows us to recognize truth and nobility. When we live in a way that fulfills this part of ourselves, we reach true happiness.

Why is Contemplation the Best Life?

- Thinking and understanding are the highest activities.
  ○ Reason is our greatest ability, and truth is the most valuable thing we can know.
- Contemplation is continuous.
  ○ Thinking and learning can go on forever. They don't need rest like other activities do.
- It brings lasting pleasure.
  ○ The joy of understanding truth is greater than the pleasure of searching for it.
- A happy life should be self-sufficient.
  ○ Justice and courage require acting with or for others.
  ○ Thinking, however, can happen alone.

Why Contemplation is Divine

If we imagine the gods, we assume they are perfectly happy. But what kind of actions would they take?

- Would they need to act bravely? No, because they face no danger.
- Would they need to be just? No, because they have no conflicts.
- Would they need to be generous? No, because they lack nothing.

So what do they do? They contemplate truth. Since contemplation is the most divine activity, it must also be the best for humans.

Even though we need basic necessities like food and shelter, true happiness does not depend on wealth or power. Even ordinary people can live well if they cultivate wisdom and virtue. The happiest life is not one of fleeting pleasure or external success, but of deep understanding. The wisest person seeks truth—not for wealth, status, or power, but because it is the most fulfilling way to live. This is why contemplation is not just good—it is the highest form of happiness..

Virtue Must Be Practiced, Not Just Understood

Now that we have explored virtue, friendship, and pleasure,

are we finished? Surely not—because knowing what is good is not enough. We must live it.

- Words can't make people virtuous. If they could, philosophy teachers would get the highest rewards.
- Most people chase pleasure and avoid pain. Reason may inspire those who are already good, but desire drives the rest.
- Those who have never experienced what is truly noble do not desire it.

For such people, reason alone is not enough—habits and laws must shape character.

Why Laws Are More Effective Than Personal Advice

If people are to live virtuously, they must follow reason and order. However:

- A father's advice lacks authority over an entire community.
- A single ruler, unless a king, does not have enough power to enforce virtue.
- Laws, however:

  ○ Command obedience.
  ○ Are based on practical wisdom.
  ○ Encourage good habits without causing personal resentment.

People often follow necessity more than reason. So, laws need to guide them, not just when they're young, but all through life.

Reflection & Application: Pleasure and Happiness

Reflection Questions

- Have you ever chased short-term pleasure at the cost of long-term happiness?
- What are some activities that bring you genuine, lasting joy instead of just quick pleasure?
- Do you agree that contemplation (deep thinking) is the highest form of happiness? Why or why not?
- How do your daily habits help shape your character? What changes could make you more virtuous?
- How can laws, culture, or education help people live more virtuous lives today?

Actionable Steps

✓ Choose joy that lasts. Some things make you happy for a moment, but real happiness comes from things that matter—like kindness, learning, and doing what's right.

✓ Build good habits. Happiness isn't just about feeling good—it comes from making good choices every day. Be kind, work hard, and treat others with respect.

✓ Spend time thinking and learning. Happiness isn't just about fun. Take time to ask big questions, read, and reflect on what really matters to you.

✓ Surround yourself with the right people. Choose friends who make you better, support your goals, and encourage you to be your best self.

✓ Balance work, rest, and purpose. Don't just work hard—make sure what you're doing has meaning. Take breaks, but use your time wisely.

✓ Follow wisdom, not just rules. Laws and traditions help guide people, but real happiness comes from understanding *why* good choices matter. Think for yourself and do what's right.

EPILOGUE

A Final Thought: From Ethics to Politics

Aristotle ends The Nicomachean Ethics with a challenge. Knowing what is good isn't enough. We must create lives and societies that promote virtue.

This idea flows into his next work, Politics. In this book, he looks at how laws, leaders, and constitutions shape human life. If *Ethics* is about how an individual should live, *Politics* is about how a society should be governed to support that life.

But the lesson remains the same: Happiness is not found in wealth or power—it is found in living wisely and virtuously.

This wraps up our modern take on *The Nicomachean*

Ethics. Aristotle's classic wisdom helps us live wisely, make good choices, and build a fulfilling life.

But the search for wisdom doesn't stop here. This book is part of the *For Everyone* series, a collection of timeless works rewritten in clear, modern language. We make history's most important ideas accessible—so you can learn from the greatest thinkers without struggling through dense, outdated text.

The *For Everyone* series explores philosophy, personal growth, and financial success—essential knowledge that has guided leaders, thinkers, and everyday people for centuries.

If you found this book helpful, be sure to explore the rest of the series. Each book makes profound insights easy to understand and apply.

Thanks for reading! Remember, wisdom isn't just for studying—it's for living. The greatest ideas from the past still have power today, and your journey toward understanding and self-improvement never ends.